Footlights
in the
Foothills

**Amateur Theatre of Las Vegas and Fort Union,
New Mexico, 1871–1899**

Footlights in the Foothills

Amateur Theatre of Las Vegas and Fort Union, New Mexico, 1871–1899

Edwina Portelle Romero

SUNSTONE PRESS

SANTA FE

Sunstone books may be purchased for educational, business, or sales promotional use.
For information please write: Special Markets Department, Sunstone Press,
P.O. Box 2321, Santa Fe, New Mexico 87504-2321.

Book and Cover design ⤶ Vicki Ahl
Body typeface ⤶ Georgia
Printed on acid free paper

Library of Congress Cataloging-in-Publication Data

Romero, Edwina Portelle, 1942-
  Footlights in the foothills : amateur theatre of Las Vegas and Fort Union, New
Mexico, 1871-1899 / by Edwina Portelle Romero.
     p. cm.
  Includes bibliographical references and index.
  ISBN 978-0-86534-826-4 (softcover : alk. paper)
  1. Amateur theater--New Mexico--Las Vegas--History--19th century. 2. Amateur
theater--New Mexido--Fort Union--History--19th century. I. Title.
  PN2277.L38R58 2011
  792.02'220978955--dc23
                              2011024462

Published in

WWW.SUNSTONEPRESS.COM
SUNSTONE PRESS / POST OFFICE BOX 2321 / SANTA FE, NM 87504-2321 /USA
(505) 988-4418 / ORDERS ONLY (800) 243-5644 / FAX (505) 988-1025

For Rachel, my daughter and my inspiration.

I regard the theatre as the greatest of all art forms,
the most immediate way in which a human being can share
with another the sense of what it is to be a human being.
—Oscar Wilde (1854–1900)

Contents

Amigos Pastores

*I*t is night, or nearly night. Grey winter light, candle-glow, lanterns, and torches cast long shadows across the snow and frozen mud. The air is crystal with dew. Horses stamp their hooves and blow steam, a few goats forage, and small groups of shawled and hooded people approach *la casa de corte*, a low *adobe* building on the north rim of *la plaza de Nuestra Señora de Dolores de Las Vegas*. The people arrive in wagons and carts, on horseback, and on foot. They enter the venerable building, which usually houses clerks and judges, and sit on the wooden benches. The air is thick with smoke and dust and the scent of burning *piñon* logs.

It is not a church, but all on the benches show a reverence for what is to come, for they are the audience.

Some people whisper—quieting children, greeting distant neighbors. Most rest their gazes ahead at the white-washed wall yellowed by candle flame, the honorable dais, and the newly added wooden platform holding a small bench and a roughhewn cradle stuffed with bits of straw. This is the set.

To one side of the stage, a group of people gathers. Ten figures in homespun robes of various shades of white and grasping tall staffs decorated with strips of colored cloth, a woman wearing a pale blue shawl and simple gown, a girl posing in white dress and veil, a boy fidgeting under his rough cloak that puddles around him on the smooth earthen floor, and one masked figure draped in black engage in animated conversation. For these are the actors.

The room fills to its capacity. Audience members shift and readjust to accommodate new comers. A baby murmurs, a woman hums softly. The shuffling of boots slows as people fill the aisles and line the side walls. The boy in the oversized robe detaches himself from the group of actors and runs to close the doors. The people watch as he weaves his way among them, crosses to the far corner, pokes the fireplace flames, and quickly rejoins the costumed group.

The actors huddle and nod, then disperse and take up positions within the set. The woman in the blue shawl, cradling a small blanketed form, sits on the bench behind the crib and bows her head. A man dressed in brown rough trousers and cloak takes his position beside her and strikes a reverent pose. The figure in black fades to the rear of the platform as The Shepherds take center stage, form two rows, and turn to face one another. The candlelight flickers. The crowd hushes to silence.

One Shepherd turns and approaches the audience. He pauses at the edge of the stage, then chants the expected greeting.

> *Amigos pastores*
> *Lla es tiempo de ver*
> *A la virgen Maria*
> *Y al Niño en Belen.*

And the play begins.

The Las Vegas Plaza, South and East Sides, ca. 1879. J. N. Furlong,
Courtesy City of Las Vegas Museum and Rough Rider Memorial
Collection, 61.2.1.

Prologue

A Pioneer Troupe, Las Vegas, The 1870s

The "Pastores" is holding forth in the community <u>sala</u>
resplendent with the soft glow of the light of kerosene lamps
braced against creamy whitewashed walls, and resounding
with the echoes of the <u>coros</u> and <u>letras</u> of the Shepherds' play.
—Aurora Lucero-White Lea

What ultimately came to be known as Las Vegas, New Mexico, began in 1821 as an agricultural land grant under the government of Spain. Fourteen years later, the Mexican government granted the seemingly abandoned area, nearly half a million acres, to a group of men from nearby San Miguel del Bado. Originally named *Nuestra Señora de los Dolores de Las Vegas*, or Our Lady of Sorrows of the Meadows, the second settlement was abandoned temporarily; however, by the spring of 1836, under orders from the Mexican government to establish a settlement, dig irrigation ditches, and plant crops, the grantees returned to the area.[1] Two towns—Las Vegas and Upper Las Vegas—were the results of their efforts.[2]

Hugging the west bank of the Gallinas River at the foothills of the *Sangre de Cristo* Mountains and teetering on the edge of the Great Plains, Las Vegas served as a key outpost on the Santa Fe Trail (ca. 1821–1880) and as a source of supplies to Fort Union (1851–91). The Trail commerce brought immigrants, speculators, soldiers, outlaws, traders, and prosperity to the area. In spite of its hard-bitten frontier environment, or perhaps because of it, the people of Las Vegas appreciated all sorts of entertainment—burlesque, folk-drama, minstrelsy, melodrama, even *opéra bouffe*—and much of it was presented by local amateurs. By day they ran shops, labored on farms and ranches, traded goods, managed large households, or provided services, but at night they donned costumes and makeup, sang solos, portrayed characters, and danced in whatever venues were available.

According to F. Stanley, entertainment on the Las Vegas *plaza* "before the American Occupation of 1846" included *fiestas,* bullfights, and at least one play: "the story of Juan Diego, El Indio, and the Virgen de Guadalupe [was] enacted each year on the twelfth of December."[3] However, one of the earliest organized amateur performing companies seems to have been

> . . .that pioneer troupe—Mariano Monclova, Pablo Gallegos, José Galindre—who gave the first [Las Vegas] performance of the play [*Los Coloquios de los Pastores*] on Christmas Eve of the year 1871 or 1872 in the courthouse where Ilfeld's warehouse now [1932] stands on Plaza Vieja . . . ."[4]

Los Pastores, as it is generally known, depicts the story of "the birth of Christ as told by the shepherds."[5]

In her thesis, *"Coloquios de los pastores de Las Vegas,"* Aurora Lucero-White provides the most comprehensive study of these pioneer thespians. Her interviews in the early 1930s with José Galindre, one of the founding members, confirms that this troupe presented the premier performance of *Los Pastores* in Las Vegas and continued performing as a company for approximately fifteen years. Galindre identified additional productions and related the story of how the "pioneer troupe" came to be. It began with Mariano Monclova, a leather craftsman.

Born in Mexico in 1838, Monclova emigrated to the Las Vegas settlement around the late 1860s and set up his trade in the *plaza vieja* area, bringing with him, *de memoria*, that is, memorized, the entire text of at least two plays—*Los Pastores* and *Adán y Eva*. Lucero-White explains that Monclova would have heard, seen, and memorized the plays during his childhood.[6]

After arriving in Las Vegas, Monclova married the sister of Pablo Gallegos. José Galindre had married another of Gallegos' sisters and thus the three men became relatives. Lucero-White believes that Monclova recited the plays at family gatherings and by 1871 or 1872, the brothers-in-law performed *Los Pastores* as well as *Adán y Eva* before a large audience in the "*Casa de Corte*" on the Las Vegas "*plaza vieja.*" Pablo Gallegos directed the production, Monclova played the shepherd Bato, and Galindre took the role of Tubal.[7]

Monclova left the Las Vegas area sometime before 1880, but Pablo Gallegos had made written copies of the two plays. Gallegos and Galindre continued producing annual performances. Lucero-White documents another performance of the two plays ca. 1883 at "*la sala que llamaban de Lorenzo Lopez,*" presently the site of Our Lady of Sorrows church rectory on Valencia Street. Some of the cast members included José Campos as Bato, Melecio Archibeque as Tebano, Doña Cornelia Galindre as Gila, Adelaido Tafoya as Angel, and José Galindre played Demonio, the Devil. Pablo Gallegos directed the production and played The Hermit. Due to high attendance numbers, the group provided a repeat performance, earning 160 *pesos* on opening night and 150 *pesos* on the following night.

Another performance of *Los Pastores* involving Gallegos and Galindre was presented at *la plaza de arriba* or Upper Las Vegas, also known as San Antonio, a few years after 1883 under the direction of Serafín Baca. For this production, group members secured José

Longino Galindre's written transcription of *Los Pastores,* as well as the production rights, for 10 *pesos.*[8] Further productions of these plays were numerous and frequent.[9] Because this performance took place ca. 1886 and because it was directed by Serafín Baca, it may represent the beginnings of the Baca Family Troupe.[10] In any event, these documented performances are several years apart; however, because the plays were performed as part of the annual Christmas celebrations and because Galindre and Gallegos were involved in the productions, it is safe to infer that this pioneer troupe performed at least once each year.

Dramatic productions of *Los Pastores* would have resembled those of European mystery plays[11] in which characters represent qualities, such as evil or piety. However, the actors donned costumes and memorized their roles. The shepherds wore long white robes and carried staffs "decorated with ribbons, tinsel and paper flowers." The actors delivered their lines as long speeches and songs rather than dialogue. In her introduction to *Los Pastores* (1940), Aurora Lucero-White Lea describes a typical performance:

> . . . *la sala* is filled to overflowing with the *gente* who have come over from the ranches and the neighboring houses to hear again for the hundredth time the story of the Borning so dear to their hearts. [They] sit through the long drawn colloquies of the shepherds couched in the elegant language of the Golden Age and interpolated with gongorisms much more unintelligible than the Latin of the [church] ritual.[12]

Although thematically connected to the Christmas story, at times, *Los Pastores* was presented in private settings such as ranch houses.[13]

In the 1870s, Las Vegas was a collection of households, farms, saloons, and commercial enterprises. Unpaved roads, candle light, and hot meals greeted weary travelers. The role Monclova, an immigrant to the Territory, played in bringing scripts as well as the impetus to perform illustrates the importance of such travel to early theatre in the American Southwest. Inconveniences did not inhibit these amateur thespians—Galindre, a laborer,[14] Monclova, a leather craftsman, and Las Vegan Pablo Gallegos. Documentation accounts for three productions spaced several years apart as well as additional numerous and frequent performances.[15] The nature and duration of the productions and their connection to the Christmas celebrations indicate continuity and organization. Continued research may uncover additional documented performances; however, religious folk-drama productions may not have been advertised or reviewed in print.[16] Based on the memories of José Galindre, these three men formed one of the first amateur performing companies of Las Vegas.

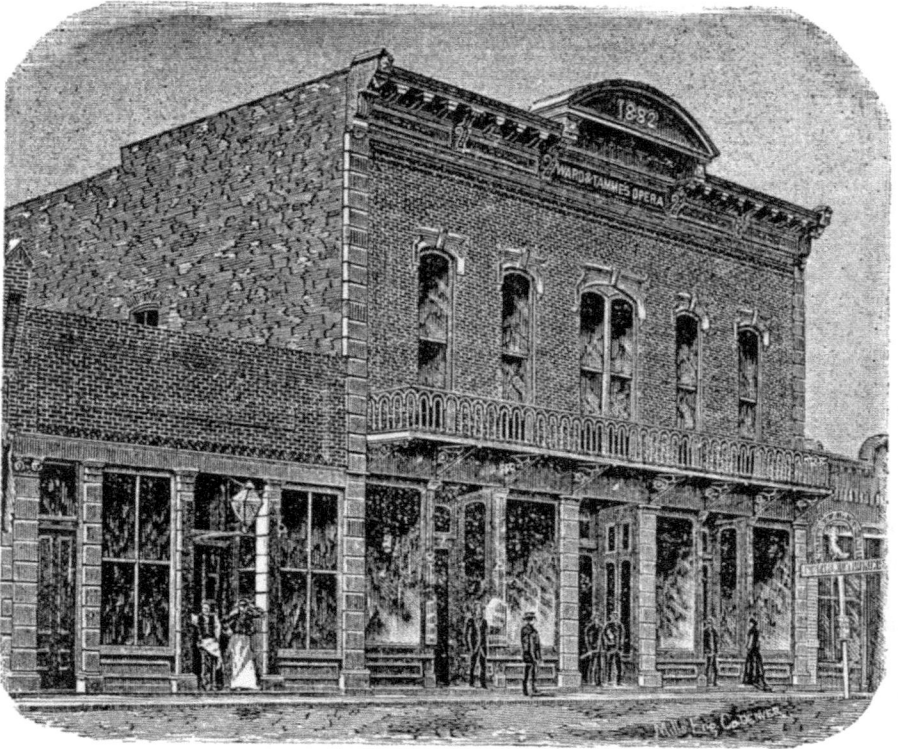

Sketch of the First Ward and Tamme Opera House, Railroad Avenue, 1882.
In Andrew K. Gregg, *New Mexico in the Nineteenth Century, A Pictorial History*.

1

A Plethora of Performances

Las Vegas, The 1880–1890s

Chapman's Hall in old Las Vegas had its first show of the season last night. The audience was quite a brilliant one and the whole affair passed off in a very enjoyable and satisfactory manner. The ladies seemed to enjoy it very much, reflecting much credit among the management.
—Las Vegas Daily Optic, 1879

On July 4, 1879, on tracks laid a few miles east of the Las Vegas trading center, the first railroad train arrived, giving birth to a new settlement. As Santa Fe Trail commerce and travelers converted to rail, the east side of the Gallinas River prospered. On July 26, a few weeks after the first locomotive rolled into the depot, the east side held opening celebrations for several "places of amusement."[1] One of the earliest buildings erected on the east side was Monarch Hall with George Ward and Charles Tamme proprietors.[2] The west side of the river maintained its status through established businesses, retail and service industries, politics, and tradition while the fledgling east side struggled with growing pains.

Because of its booming economy, Las Vegas drew a variety of traveling entertainment companies but continued to nurture home talent. By the 1880s, the communities on both sides of the Gallinas River sported opera houses and performance halls. Some enterprising saloon keepers saw the advantages of adding performance spaces: "In 1893, the owners of the Elite Bar fixed up a miniature theater with one hundred seats."[3] Many of the early halls were on the west side. Chapman's Hall was located at 125 and 127 Bridge Street, and Felix Papa's Hall was inside the Exchange Hotel on the *plaza*.[4] Also located on the plaza were the Imperial Hall, owned and managed by Vicente Silva, and an establishment run by Chata Baca, "a robust woman who enforced strict discipline" among her girls although a visitor "described her hall as 'a low, mud dance house thick with tobacco smoke, rum breath, fumes of perspiration, and adobe dust.'" At that time, the word *hall* might refer to any facility "large enough for [the] promotion of public, commercialized dancing" as well as libations and gambling.[5]

In addition to halls and saloons, the 1880s saw the rise of opera houses. The Ward-Tamme Opera House on Railroad Avenue opened in 1882 and was considered spacious, "airy and comfortable" although at times, extra chairs were needed to accommodate the crowds.[6] Due to the success of the Ward-Tamme, in 1886, Charles Tamme opened a second, larger, and more impressive opera house on the corner of Douglas Avenue and Sixth Street with a seating capacity of over 800. The building also housed offices, shops, a café, and an "elegantly furnished" saloon. For the House's opening events, with close to 400 patrons attending, Fort Union's Tenth Infantry Band and a local orchestra conducted by Carlos Curti performed.[7] By 1897, the Tamme Opera House had become the Duncan Opera House.[8] At least one additional establishment, Mackel's Opera House, was located next to Buffalo Hall on the southwest side of the *plaza* but was destroyed in the 1912 fire.[9] J. B. Mackel, who had once operated a liquor and tobacco establishment inside Buffalo Hall, also built Mackel's Pavilion at the triangle of Grand and Douglas Avenues.[10]

In spite of its budding sophistication, Las Vegas was definitely a frontier town. At one point, a Colonel McClure rented one of the performance venues, the Globe Theatre, to store hay and grain.[11] Consequently, playing Las Vegas must have been an adventure, and for amateurs, it could have been downright daunting. When the venue was not stocked with feed, the audience might include not only the editors of the daily newspapers and members of the local, self-proclaimed, aristocracy but also rough wranglers and impertinent outlaws. Doc Holliday operated a dentist's office and/or saloon—the exact nature of the business is unclear—on Lincoln Avenue; the Silva gang terrorized the area from about 1875–1894 with robberies, cattle-rustling, and murder;[12] and on December 26, 1880, Dave Rudabaugh and Billy the Kid spent a night in the Las Vegas jail. The next morning, Pat Garret and his deputies held off a gang of vigilantes who wanted to hang Rudabaugh for the murder of Las Vegas jailer Lino Valdez.[13] By 1881, Las Vegas had acquired a reputation as "the toughest town on the Western frontier."[14]

Given the general ambience of the area, local audiences ran the gamut from vocally enthusiastic to rudely unwelcoming. In 1886, visiting professional actress Grace Hawthorne walked off the stage in mid-performance because "a gang of hoodlums" was making so much noise that the manager, Charles Tamme, and Marshal Jilson were called upon to establish order.[15] The following year, Haydon Tilla, a "world renowned tenor," canceled his lecture and performance due to a small turn-out."[16] Twelve years later, things were no better:

> At a home talent play in 1899 the director had to stop the performance and threaten to call the police in order to get twenty young men of 'the best families' to cease their rowdiness and depart from the auditorium.[17]

Popular theatrical fare of the day—bawdy, boisterous, and often spontaneous—may have encouraged rowdiness among audience members. R. A. Kistler, the editor of the *Las Vegas Daily Optic,* described "The Female Bathers," performed at a hall on the west side, as "one of the naughtiest acts we have ever seen."[18] Monte Verde, the beautiful dark-eyed brunette, lavishly dressed in velvet and diamonds[19] and identified as the famous Confederate spy Belle Siddons, performed a variety and vaudeville act at the Globe Theatre in East Las Vegas. Later she "opened 'the Parlor,' a palace of pleasure, on Sixth street" where she performed banjo solos and was considered a "leading variety lady."[20]

One indication of local concern about the content of productions is emphasized in an article related to The Holman Troupe, a traveling company. On Tuesday, December 9, 1879, the Troupe appeared at Chapman's Hall, and a talented local performer spontaneously joined the group onstage. M. Hirsch "volunteered to do a turn on this occasion, and there are no amateurs that can do so well as he." In the brief *Optic* review, it was made clear that this production was not for the rowdy: "The most Puritanical could not take offense at anything that was said or done last night."[21]

In the spring of 1880, the editor of the *Optic* bemoaned the lack of amateur theatricals, or possibly he was challenging the community to what he believed to be higher standards:

> It occurred to us that Vegas is needful of one thing she has not, but which she could easily possess by turning over her hand. And that is a theatrical company of home talent—such as other towns have and support.[22]

By 1885, Pat Garrett and his family were living in Las Vegas,[23] the third Montezuma Hotel—said to have cost a million dollars—was built,[24] a fifty-eight foot high pipe organ was installed at Our Lady of Sorrows Church,[25] and several home talent groups were answering Kistler's call. Some companies, like the Baca Family Troupe, the Las Vegas Comedy Company, and the Las Vegas Opera Company, left enduring marks on the theatrical landscape while others came and went quickly or were organized for a specific purpose such as fundraising or school recitals. Although documentation on these latter groups is minimal, highlights of their presentations broaden the perspective on 19th century amateur productions in the area.

On February 26, 1885, at the Ward-Tamme Opera House on Railroad Avenue, the Las Vegas Comedy Company, under the leadership of W. H. Leroy, presented "the laughable and popular comedy; 'Uncle Josh Whitcomb,'"[26] based on Denman Thompson's (1833–1911) sketch of a salty New England farmer. In his 1875 vaudeville performance of "Uncle Josh," Thompson created a stock character referred to as the "'rube,' a burlesque of the rural working class." With its commentaries on the tensions between rural ideals and the demands of American industrialization, this character type remained popular well into the 20th century[27] and knew no regional boundaries. In 1878, Thompson created a short play, *Joshua Whitcomb,* and in 1887, his four-act play, *The Old Homestead* opened.[28] Because the Las Vegas performance took place in 1885, it must have been a rendition of the earlier play, *Joshua Whitcomb.*

A preview in the *Optic* of February 24th provided the cast of characters. The leading role, Uncle Josh, was played by Will E. Curtis; Miss Annie Lisenbee portrayed a street sweeper; Miss Carrie Hume played Nellie Primrose; and W. H. Leroy directed the performance and took the role of John Martin, a Bostonian.[29] Billed as "180 Laughs in 180 Minutes," admission was $1.00 for reserved seating and $.75 general admission.[30]

On February 27th, an anonymous reviewer declared that the troupe was "an eminently amateurish confederation" but that there was a "good-sized audience" and there would be another performance that evening. The reviewer noted that the presentation was

> . . . somewhat better than that turned out on the same boards by professional barnstormers. In the cast were rising lights of the class to which belong such people as . . . Lottie [Lotta] Crabtree.[31]

Charlotte Crabtree (1847–1924), known as Lotta, was one of America's most popular and successful entertainers. Tutored by Lola Montez, Crabtree sang, acted, danced, and played the banjo,[32] so to be compared to her was praise indeed. However, the reviewer bemoaned the cost of tickets: "Give us cheaper seats and take bigger houses to entertain,"[33] and on March 3, the Company responded with another performance for fifty cents. Sadly, this was the troupe's final effort in Las Vegas due to the loss of Will E. Curtis who departed for "the East."[34] Nine years later, the name, Las Vegas Comedy Company, would resurface under the direction of Alexander Randolph.

On March 12, 1886, the Spanish Comedy Company presented an evening of theatrical productions, vocal entertainment, and dances. In Felix Papa's Hall at the Exchange Hotel, this ambitious group, with " befitting and expensive costumes," performed *El Medico a Palos,"* a very laughable production indeed,"[35] followed by *The Afflicted, The Cowboy,* and *The Valient* [sic.] *Man.* After the first play, group members presented "a Spanish dance, and following the second play, Miss Lucero performed "a song rendered in most pleasing and effective style." Players included José Pereida, Demetrio Silva, Felicia Montoya, Catarina Sandoval, Adolfo Sandoval, Irene Solano, Luis Ulibarri, and George Bruno. Ezequiel C. de Baca, who would serve as New Mexico state governor in 1917, performed in all four plays and was reported to have danced with Miss Montoya. According to a review in the *Las Vegas Daily Gazette,* "the audience went home fully satisfied."[36] The Company gave its final performance of the season at Felix Papa's Hall on April 1st with an evening of five plays:

> El Truvador, a drama in three acts; Los Ciegos Fingidos, the pretended blind men; La Carta Perdida, the lost letter; Los Alcaldes Chasquiados, the deceived judges; the whole to conclude with the operetta, La Viuda y el Sacristan, the widow and the priest.[37]

The time period of the Spanish Comedy Company productions coincides with the beginnings of the Baca Family Troupe and the Spanish-language *sociedades de ayuda,* confirming the existence of intense literary and dramatic activities in support of the Spanish language as described later in this chapter.

Throughout the 1880s and 90s, the term *local talent* appeared in the newspapers; however, because of grammatical inconsistencies, it is not clear when the phrase was used to designate an organized troupe or simply a generic gathering of local amateurs. Three productions attributed to "local talent" illustrate the range of Las Vegas's amateur performers as well as their abilities to come together and produce much appreciated performances.

In the appendix of her thesis, "Footlights in the Foothills: A History of the Las Vegas, New Mexico, Opera Houses," Dorothy LeGault lists two performances of *The Reign of the Fairies* at the Tamme Opera House on May 6 and 7, 1885, by "Local Talent," capitalized but in parenthesis.[38] However, a search of the Las Vegas newspapers revealed no previews, reviews, or advertisements, and a broader search for information on the play, itself, was fruitless.

Eight years later, on July 1,1893, another group referred to as "Local Talent" presented a three-act drama, *Nevada or the Lost Mine*, written in 1882 by George M. Baker (1832–1890).[39] According to a review in the *Las Vegas Daily Optic*, the play was "well-rendered, the amateurs engaged in it showing considerable talent and commendable practice." However, attendance was low—the "smallest in fact given a home entertainment. . . ."[40]

In 1897, "local talent" presented a program for Saint Patrick's Day at the Duncan Opera House on Douglas Avenue. The production included recitations, a whistle solo, and the operetta, *Gypsy Queen*. Miss Josephine O'Keefe and Mrs. Sallie Douglas, assisted by Professor Charles Rumley, directed the program. The cast ranged in ages from two years to "grown young ladies."

An *Optic* reviewer proclaimed, "Las Vegas certainly has more fine talent than any other two towns of its size in the United States" and singled out several members of the cast. The Misses Carrie and Perle Wean as the Gypsy Queen and Rosalie respectively "were unsurpassed." Furthermore, "these young ladies possess unusual talent and musical and dramatic ability." The writer also noted that "the concert programme was delightfully rendered" and included a mandolin solo by Miss McMurtry, vocal solos by Mr. Hofmeister and Miss Blanche Rothgeb, an ocarina solo by Mr. Eckert, and the violin playing of Miss Beatrice Atkins and Miss Edith Rothgeb.[41]

Some of the actors in this performance had clear ties to the community and performed with other local companies. Gustave A. Rothgeb held an interest in the Las Vegas Brewing Company at the corner of Gonzales and Delgado west of the *plaza*.[42] Blanche, Pearl, and Edith Rothgeb appeared in many amateur productions and often provided supporting performances for traveling professionals. Blanche sang a solo at a local performance of Jessie Couthoui, a "Popular Recitationist,"[43] and Edith served as First Violinist with Max Nordhaus's orchestra.[44] In addition to performing vocal solos, Louis Hofmeister conducted "a first class, family grocery" on Bridge Street.[45]

However, according to the *Optic* review of March 18, 1897, the children stole the show: "The recitation, 'I'd rather be a boy,' by Bertha, the little infant daughter of Mr. and Mrs. Cohen, brought down the house and forced an encore." A dance by Nellie, the daughter of Mr. and Mrs. M. C. Drury, was "wonderfully beautiful" as were the dances by Mattie Weller and Maggie Burks, and "Miss Damacia Montoya delighted the audience with a piano solo."

Although the performance was a grand success, a problem regarding the seating arrangements "was greatly regretted, but the stage full of gypsies, and fairies and the beautiful scenery were a delight to all." By request, the group gave a repeat performance on March 20 at Rosenthal Hall, formerly the Ward-Tamme Opera House on Railroad Avenue. At the second show, a "children's programme" and a dance were added. Admission for the entire production was twenty-five cents for adults and fifteen cents for children.[46] Although not identified as such, this production may have represented a music or dramatic school recital rather than that of a fully organized theatre company; hence, the meaning of the term *local talent* remains illusive.

One unusually large and ambitious amateur production received the exuberant attention of the *Optic*. On January 9 and 11, 1886, "under the auspices and for the benefit of Thomas Post No. 1, G. A. R."

75 amateurs, directed by the author, Colonel E. B. Temple, presented *Union Spy*. Advertised as "A Complete History of the Great Rebellion in one Night," this production about the American Civil War was performed at the Ward and Tamme Opera House[47] on Railroad Avenue.

According to the *Optic*, the performance "was extremely successful, no less in respect of attendance than in the rendering of the play. The house was crowded to repletion with the intelligent and social distinction of the city." However, the reviewer noted that the subject matter might have affected audience members personally, "rendering them insensitive to the niceties of the delineation. And no doubt a less successful interpretation would have been received with applause"[48] In 1862, a major Civil War battle, as well as several skirmishes, had occurred at nearby Glorieta Pass when 400 Fort Union soldiers encountered and defeated four companies of invading Confederate troupes. "Considering the total number [of men] involved in the battle, it had been a bloody affair."[49]

Although reluctant to criticize individual performances because of the size of the cast, the reviewer stated that "each and all exceeded in the parts [and] assumed the most friendly expectation." These amateur actors realistically depicted scenes of Civil War battlefields, a lonely sentinel, a bivouac of thousands, and "loathsome" prison cells. "The San Miguel rifles . . . acquitted themselves with a trained and soldierly exactness noteworthy of veterans." The writer also pointed out that the character of Uncle Tom provided "a world of fun for the small boys" and that the tableaux were well-posed while "many . . .were truly beautiful."[50] A large part of 19th century minstrel show performance included and was drawn from Black America's minstrel tradition and stock characters[51] much like Uncle Josh Whitcomb's "rube," a White American counterpart to Uncle Tom.

Union Spy was available for fundraising and was produced in various parts of the country using local amateurs, especially military or militia veterans. In Hancock County, OH, community amateurs, including a "military company of old soldiers," raised $600 to complete a monument to its Civil War casualties,[52] and in St. Paul, MN, the

Acker Post of the Grand Army of the Republic devoted one fifth of its proceeds from producing this play to "the benefit of the Home for the Friendless."[53] However, the *Optic* reviewer felt that the Las Vegas performance was special: "we doubt if it [the play] was ever rendered in a town of this size, and wholly by amateurs, more successfully than in Las Vegas."[54]

Several years later, on Thursday, July 5, 1894, at the Tamme Opera House, a group calling itself the Las Vegas Dramatic Company produced the Civil War drama, *The Woven Web* (1889) by Charles Townsend.[55] The cast of this "Four Act Melo-Drama," included the names of several local amateurs. Max Nordhaus, who had studied music in Germany and was a brother-in-law of Charles Ilfeld,[56] directed the orchestra, and Edith Rothgeb served as first violinist. Both names appear in the cast listings of programs for the Las Vegas Opera Company and the Oratorio Society. Clearly, Las Vegas amateurs lent their skills to any and all performance opportunities.

The *Optic* reviewer favorably compared the Dramatic Company players to professionals, stating that the performance "was one of the most creditable ever given by local and amateur talent, in this city." The drama involved unrequited love, a villain, an Irish servant, and both Yankees and Confederates. The "make-up was natural," and the performers were "unusually correct; their acting not overdone, and their enunciation agreeably distinct." However, the reporter, apparently following the newspaper's policy, refused to engage in theatrical analysis or criticism:

> To draw distinctions, where all did so well, would be invidious: and THE OPTIC will only add that Messrs. Cluxton, York, Cavanaugh, Ilfeld, Mennet, and Hollingsworth, and Misses Harkness, Lay, and Campbell, [sic.] gave an entertainment which all enjoyed, and of which the city is justly proud as a local production.[57]

One of the significant features of amateur theatre is its involvement in and reflection of community. When rail service arrived in Las Vegas, it brought many new people of diverse ethnicities and races and thus, strengthened "ethnic consciousness" among the *Nuevo Mexicanos*. As a result, Spanish-language newspapers, featuring sections on literature, poetry, and popular fiction, flourished. Literary and dramatic societies, whose ranks included prominent citizens like Ezequiel C. de Baca, organized specifically for educational purposes. These *sociedades* held debates, supported charities, established a Spanish-language library, and sponsored amateur theatrical productions in Spanish.[58]

The acting groups associated with the *sociedades* focused on enhancing the use of the Spanish language. In November of 1891, *la Sociedad Literaría y de Ayuda Mutual de Las Vegas,* one of the first such organizations in the territory, established an amateur theatrical counterpart, *la Sociedad Dramática Hispano-Americano.*[59] Additional Spanish-language companies in the Las Vegas area included *La Sociedad Dramática* and *El Club Dramático de Las Vegas.*[60]

On January 30, 1892, *La Sociedad Dramática Hispano-Americano* presented an evening of dramas. A reviewer in *La Voz del Pueblo* complimented the actors on the fine interpretations of their roles but criticized the quality of the plays and reported that soon the group would receive new comedies from Mexico City.[61] Later that month, *el Club Dramático*, made up of members of *la Sociedad de San Juan*, gathered a large audience on Saturday, February 27, for another selection of short plays. All the plays were deemed excellent, except *Medias Zuelas y Tacones*—loosely translated—*Half Soles and Heels*. According to the brief review, *el Club* would resume production after lent, and it was hoped that with more practice, some of the actors would achieve *"la perfección."*[62]

The Las Vegas settlements supported a large number of amateur companies and their diverse performance offerings. These companies produced short sketches, full length plays, variety shows, and musical entertainments. They played in undependable venues to erratic and sometimes rowdy audiences. But thanks to these irrepressible thespians, the community enjoyed a wide variety of works from American, English, Irish, Mexican, and Spanish playwrights.

TAMME OPERA HOUSE,
East Las Vegas,
Saturday Evening, April the 12th, 1890.

Extraordinary presentation of the charming Japanese Comic Opera,
in two acts,

The Little Tycoon,
— BY —
THE · LAS · VEGAS · OPERA · COMPANY.

UNDER THE DIRECTION OF
PROFESSOR JOHN A. HAND, Jr.

Cast.

Gen. Knickerbocker	Mr. D. T. Hoskins
Alvin Barry	Mr. H. J. O'Bryan
Rufus Reddy	Mr. J. Combs
Lord Dolphin	Mr. J. D. O'Bryan, Jr.
Teddy	Mr. Ned Gross
Officer	Mr. C. B. Eads
Montgomery	Mr. T. LaRue
Foreman	Mr. B. Wilson
Miss Hurricane	Miss Josie Parsons
Dolly Dimple	Miss Blanche Rothgeb
Violet	Miss Hattie Knickerbocker

CHORUS OF JAPANESE — CHORUS OF BRIGANDS
CHORUS OF HOBGOBLINS — CHORUS OF TOURISTS

Scenes.

ACT I.—Back of Ocean Steamer returning from Europe.
ACT II.—Drawing Room in Gen. Knickerbocker's Villa, and Transformation
Scene into Garden of Gen. Knickerbocker's Home.

MEMBERS OF LAS VEGAS OPERA CO.

Miss Blanche Rothgeb	Mr. H. J. O'Bryan
Miss Josie Parsons	Mr. J. D. O'Bryan, Jr.
Miss Hattie Knickerbocker	Mr. Ned Gross
Mrs. M. A. Otero	Mr. J. Combs
Mrs. H. J. O'Bryan	Mr. D. T. Hoskins
Miss Virginia Atkins	Mr. M. A. Otero
Miss Maid Neff	Mr. F. J. Thomas
Miss May Halpin	Mr. A. E. North
Miss May Keller	Mr. Chas. Moore
Miss Mack Keller	Mr. W. Thomas
Miss Mary LaRue	Mr. A. Mennet, Jr.
Miss Maggie Lee	Mr. L. B. Allan
Miss Mary Yearle	Mr. W. J. Pennebaker
Miss Nellie Malboeuf	Mr. B. Olney
Miss Beatrice Atkins	Mr. G. B. Eads
Mr. T. LaRue	Mr. B. Wilson
Mr. L. Hofheldter	

Argument.

"The Little Tycoon" is a satire on the foreign title worship craze.

General Knickerbocker has a beautiful daughter, Violet, who he determines shall make a brilliant match. Violet is in love with Alvin Barry, a young American of splendid family, whom she meets at Venice.

Returning from Europe on the same steamer is a high-toned English Lord—Lord Dolphin, with his valet, Teddy. The Lord's title completely captures the General, and he pays great court to "His Lordship," determining Violet shall marry him. All on the steamer sympathize with Alvin and Violet. Lord Dolphin, to get Alvin out of the way, procures his arrest on the charge of smuggling, and the curtain falls on the separation of the lovers.

Act second finds Violet in tears and closely guarded in her father's villa at Newport. Alvin, disguised as Lord Dolphin, gains distinguished entrance to the Knickerbocker villa, but is discovered and has to beat a hasty retreat. As a final ruse he plays on the General's great weakness—love of title, worship—and personates the Great Tycoon of Japan, thereby winning Violet and making her "The Little Tycoon."

Souvenir Program, *The Little Tycoon*. Courtesy City of Las Vegas Museum and Rough Rider Memorial Collection, 2010.1.4.

30

2

Divas, Melodramas and Troupers

Las Vegas, The 1880s–1890s

All the world's a stage,
And all the men and women merely players;
They have their exits and their entrances,
And one man in his time plays many parts,
—William Shakespeare

Beginning with the mid-1880s, three radically different amateur companies dominated the theatrical world of Las Vegas. The Baca Troupe, sometimes referred to as the Baca Family Troupe (ca. 1886–1920), provided Spanish and Mexican folk-dramas; the Las Vegas Opera Company (1885–1890s) brought lavish and comical operettas; and the Las Vegas Comedy Company (1894–1895) offered British and American melodramas. All three were equally important and popular, but because it received extensive newspaper coverage, there is more information on the doings of the Opera Company.

The first of these, the Baca Troupe, was an enduring performance group clustered around family and community. Although it became a traveling company and achieved regional popularity, the Troupe began in Las Vegas, possibly evolving from the "pioneer troupe" of the 1870s. John Englekirk believes that the group was "organized by Serafín Baca sometime in the mid-1880's" and continued performing beyond the turn of the century.[1] As with many amateur companies, documentation is scarce, so establishing specific dates is somtimes problematic. Lucero-White's interviews with José Galindre reveal that around 1886 Serafín Baca directed performances of *Los Pastores* and *Adán y Eva* in Upper Town Las Vegas with members of the pioneer troupe.[2] It is possible that Serafíin Baca was a member of the "pioneer troupe;" however, this may also represent either a collaborative effort or the debut of the Baca Troupe as a separate company. In any event, 1886 was a pivotal year for the Baca family. Many manuscripts that became part of the Troupe's repertoire originated in 1886. For the ca. 1886 Upper Town performance, Serafín Baca used José Longino Galindre's handwritten copies of *los Pastores* and *Adán y Eva* dated January 11 to February 20, 1886, and several additional manuscripts in the Troupe's repertoire were "copied directly from Mexican editions in the library of La Sociedad Literaría y de Ayuda Mutua of Las Vegas, incorporated under state Law in 1886."[3]

Once established, the Baca Troupe performed regularly in Las Vegas and expanded its horizons, spreading theatre throughout New Mexico Territory to "Mora and Taos upon the occasion of their [sic.] triumphal tour during the winter of 1903–04."[4] In essence, its members became dramatic, albeit amateur, *trovadores*.

Although the Troupe achieved Territorial popularity, it had strong ties to Las Vegas's pioneer amateur group through both Serafín Baca and his son, Próspero S. Baca (1875–1962). In his youth, Próspero performed in the "pioneer troupe" productions of *los Pastores* and "finally was established as the best St. Michael of the annual play, which was directed by Pablo Gallegos." Years later, Próspero Baca directed performances of *Los Pastores* as well as *Los Matachines*. He lived, worked, and produced amateur theatre in Las Vegas until 1922 when he and his family moved to Bernalillo.[5] In 1910, Baca listed his occupation as farmer at Agua Zarca, a now-deserted village in San Miguel County,[6] and by 1918 he was employed with the Las Vegas Commercial Club.[7] Although he remained an amateur impresario, Baca was responsible for preserving much of New Mexico's rich literary heritage as well as adding his own compositions. He passed on his love of drama and literature to the next generation through his daughter Andrellita who composed original verses until her death in 1946.[8]

The Baca Family Troupe had a significant impact on New Mexico's amateur performance groups. Carrying on the traditions of the "pioneer troupe," the Baca's performed folk-dramas in Spanish and transcribed many heretofore oral scripts, increasing the number of plays available for performance as well as preserving them for future generations. The Baca Troupe included nine secular and four non-secular plays in its repertoire.[9] Próspero Baca "copied and recopied most of the plays by hand in three different diaries."[10] One of the secular plays, *Representación de la Corte del Rey Arturo*, was "transcribed from the copy of Ezequiel C. de Baca, president of the Sociedad Literaria y de Ayuda Mutua. . . ." The Troupe rarely presented the King Arthur play, but Próspero Baca saw it performed "at least once in Las Vegas at about the turn of the [nineteenth] century."[11] *Rey Arturo* is not related to the British legend of King Arthur but rather based on the "Christian vs. Moor theme."[12]

The Baca Family Troupe spread its talent and repertoire of plays throughout the territory, enhancing and reinforcing the use of the Spanish language and the *Nuevo Mexicano* perspective as well as entertaining the people and preserving Spanish and Mexican folk-dramas. The family's culture of performance provided a model for Próspero S. Baca, who dedicated his life to collecting and conserving early folk-dramas, songs, and poems.[13]

In an entertainment milieu that welcomed folk-drama, minstrel shows, and bawdy comedies, the illustrious, ambitious, and, perhaps, pretentious Las Vegas Opera Company emerged. The Company took shape through social and business connections, and it seems, every meeting, rehearsal, or performance was covered in the Las Vegas newspapers. In addition to bringing light opera and heavy costumes to Las Vegas audiences, the group provided fundraising activities and support for budding local performers.

According to Miguel A. Otero, Jr., a member of the local business community who later served as Territorial Governor from 1897 through 1906, Las Vegas had considerable musical and performing talent and sometime around 1884 several members of what he once referred to as the "silk stocking brigade" formed the basis of the Company.[14] In his memoir, *My Life on the Frontier 1882–1897*, Otero recalled that he often met with a small group of "like-minded" people, and "it was not long before we organized an amateur opera company."[15]

Some of the founding members in addition to Otero included his sister Maimie and brother Page, D. H. Rust, Harry J. O'Bryan, Jacob and Caroline Gross, Hattie Knickerbocker, May G. Dunlop, and Emily Tetard.[16] Mrs. Caroline Gross, whom Otero nicknamed "Sister Carrie," played piano and "had a pleasing contralto voice."[17] In later years, John A. Hand, Jr., "from Chicago, a very high class musician,"[18] joined the company as musical director. Hand, often referred to as Professor, operated Hand's Music School on Bridge Street where he taught "Piano, Violin and all Stringed Instruments."[19]

The Las Vegas Opera Company provided entertainment as well as a venue for social interaction and making important business and political contacts. From 1879 to 1886, Jacob Gross and Miguel Otero, Jr. managed the San Miguel National Bank together,[20] and Gross shared his business skills with Otero.[21] The two men also shared duties among the leadership of a local vigilante group which aimed to rid Las Vegas of its "scourge of crime."[22] Company rehearsals, organizational meetings, and performances were regularly reported in local newspapers:

The rehearsal of the Home Opera company at the Plaza Hotel last night, [sic.] was attended by every member of the company except one. Rapid progress is making, and the company bid fair to give one of the best entertainments ever presented to the citizens of Las Vegas by home talent. The rehearsal tonight will be at Mrs. Judge O'Brien's at 8 o'clock.[23]

Otero claimed that, aside from providing important business contacts, the "rehearsals were great fun and always ended with a midnight supper, including plenty to eat and drink." He made it clear, however, that the organization was somewhat exclusive, its members representing what he termed the "aristocracy of East Las Vegas."[24] At that time, 1885, the town of Las Vegas consisted of the *plaza* area. The "east side was not incorporated until 1888,"[25] so Otero's use of the term "East Las Vegas" is either hindsight or a geographical designation. However, exclusive as it may have been, the Company provided much-desired and elegant productions.

The Las Vegas Opera Company made its performance debut on June 1, 1885 at the Ward and Tamme Opera House on Railroad Avenue with *The Doctor of Alcantara* (1866), an *opéra bouffe*, that is, a "satirical comic opera,"[26] by Benjamin E. Woolf (d. 1901) and Julius Eichberg (1824–1893).[27] Professor D. Boffa directed the production, which was "rendered by local talent."[28] Frank T. Robinson, a tailor with Peters and Trout's,[29] played Carlos and Mrs. Jacob Gross portrayed his lover. The *Optic* reviewer professed that "never before had the audience been so grandly entertained by an amateur company" and singled out Mrs. Sampson, stating that she brought down the house with her solos of "Oh, woe is me" and "Bolero."

Her trill on the high notes and the ease with which she took and sustained those extremely high and pure tones, was both artistic and beautiful, and caused a spontaneous burst of applause in the midst of her solo.[30]

Between the acts, Jacob Gross presented Professor Boffa with a "fine gold headed cane," and after the performance, the entire company traveled across town to the Plaza Hotel for a reception and banquet.[31]

The following year, on Saturday, March 6,1886, the Opera Company presented *Chilpéric* (1868), another *opéra bouffe*, by Hervé (1825–1892),[32] to a "large, appreciative [audience] . . . composed of the best people of Las Vegas."[33] Clearly, the reviewer was impressed, stating that rarely did one see an opening-night, amateur production "in which the stage work progressed as smoothly. The costumes would defy the descriptive powers of any but an expert."[34] Admission prices varied: "$1 for front reserved seats, 75c for middle reserved seats, and 50c for rear seats unreserved."[35]

Some individual performances were singled out. Frank Robinson played King Chilpéric: "His clear, distinct, well modulated tones, [sic.] and the perfect ease with which every syllable can be heard and fully understood, [sic.] will always make his singing a favorite with the people." Among the female performers, Mrs. Sampson "showed superior control and compass;" and for her acting, Mrs. Jacob Gross "received the largest meed of praise." The reviewer stated, "the fact is every one [sic.] did as well as could be done; and any adverse criticism would only be hypercritical."[36]

Apparently, *Chilpéric* was performed on March 6, 7, 8, and 9, 1886. Pinning down performance dates is sometimes problematic. Advertisements for this operetta noted the performances as March 6 and 7,[37] but a March 7th review in the *Las Vegas Gazette* encouraged people to attend "tomorrow night," March 8th, indicating an additional performance; furthermore, a review in the March 9th *Gazette* noted that the final performance would take place that evening and following the performance "a social dance will be given, Prof. Boffa's orchestra furnishing the music."[38] In this instance, the venue referred to would have been the Tamme Opera House on Railroad Avenue as the new Tamme Opera House on Douglas Avenue did not open until September of that year.[39]

It appears that the show on the 8th was excellent and "encores were distributed without partiality. For an amateur presentation the cast is remarkable . . . ." Several individual members received praise: General Director Schoonmaker, Clifford O'Bryan, Harry O'Bryan, Mrs. Gross, Mrs. Sampson, W. B. Scott, Frank Robinson, J. H. Ponder, Miss Cavanaugh, and Professor Boffa and his orchestra.[40]

On January 18, 1887, the Company focused on "that delightful little opera, *Billee Taylor*" (1880) by Edward Solomon (1855–1895) and Henry P. Stevens (1851–1903).[41] A January 19th review in the *Optic* signed Canto, stated that only balcony seating was available as the curtain rose on a "revelation of brilliancy and beauty." Canto mentioned Manager Tamme, indicating that the evening took place at the Tamme Opera House. The review oozes with hyperbole from the "array of lovely faces," to the "manly forms and handsome countenances," to "eminently beautiful" costumes, a set "in good taste," and "a volume of round, melodious tone." Canto also praised the orchestra with Professor Boffa as 1st violinist, Max Nordhaus at the piano, and Carlos Curti waving the baton. The stage management was praised, and the audience was deemed "eminently well behaved, well dressed, and well pleased."[42] In highlighting individual performers, Canto proclaimed Miss Mamie Parsons was "an actress to the manor born;" Dr. Rust as the "virtuous gardener . . . sang his vegetable song excellently;" and Mrs. J. Gross "fully sustained her reputation and popularity as an actress and vocalist:"

> . . . the No! No! duet with Billee was a gem. The entrance of the charity girls, led in graceful movements by Miss Otero and Miss Emmett, was the signal for deserved applause. The reporter's heart was completely captured by the grace and beauty of the thirty young ladies, the flowers of Las Vegas.[43]

Canto also highlighted performances by May Dunlop, Harriet Knickerbocker, Louis Hofmeister, Ernest L. Brown, and the "Chorus of Sailors."[44] Miguel A. Otero, Jr. was a member of the chorus.[45]

Canto's review noted that there would be an additional performance on the following Friday, January 21, and that the group was contemplating an appearance in Albuquerque: "the company will probably go down the road; at least we all hope that such will be the decision." He closed with a call for more local productions: "Let us have now a permanent opera company and performances monthly. Such a project will meet with hearty support from our people of taste and wealth."[46]

An interesting aside involves Harry O'Bryan. In his memoirs, Miguel Otero, Jr. includes a section about this production of *Billee Taylor* stating that Harry J. O'Bryan had been "assigned" to play Captain Flapper but took ill with typhoid fever. Page Otero, Miguel's brother, stepped into the part and apparently "acquitted himself splendidly and to the complete gratification" of the musical staff— Carlos Curti, Max Nordhaus, and Professor Motta.[47] However, Canto's January 19th review praises Harry O'Bryan as part of the stage management group.

For the second performance, on the 21st,[48] Canto's review, "Criticisms of Billee Taylor," took on a more instructive and critical perspective:

> The critic who could or would sit down and tear to pieces such a performance as that given by our charming young ladies and noble young gentlemen, would be mean enough to whip his mother-in-law, if he had one. Such is not the character of THE OPTIC'S correspondent who was once young himself. But it is a duty to mention some defect that can easily be avoided hereafter.[49]

In counterpoint to his review of opening night, Canto noted, Doctor Rust "should take more of his personality upon the stage and Miss Knickerbocker less;" "Louis Hoffmister [sic.] should stop singing with his mouth;" "Mrs. Gross needs vocal culture;" "Page Otero needs strength, flexibility and certainty;" and "Miss Parsons needs but one suggestion. 'Don't over-do.'" However, Canto acknowledged that both Rust and Knickerbocker had improved "in action" and that Page Otero sang more freely and confidently. Canto also included personal observations of the audience and a short, fill-in-the-blanks quiz, perhaps as a teaching tool for audience members:

> The best looking gentleman was beyond doubt Mr. _____.
> The fluent voice and best appearance among the characters is certainly that of _____.
> Mr. _____ is a mere stick.
> Miss _____flirted desperately.[50]

By 1890, John A. Hand, Jr. was directing the Company's efforts. On Monday, April 8, advertised as the Las Vegas Opera Club, the group presented *The Little Tycoon* (1886) by Willard Spenser (1852–1933)[51] at the Tamme Opera House. In a preview article, "'Little Tycoon' This Evening," the *Optic* writer proclaimed that it would be "the finest ever [performance] given in New Mexico by an amateur organization." The reporter also noted that new scenery had arrived and that the performance was sold out with "standing room, only" available.[52]

Based on the glowing review in the following day's *Optic,* the Company did not disappoint:

> Last evening the Las Vegas opera company gave an entertainment at Tamme opera house which *The Optic* does not hesitate to say was the most notable musical event in the history of New Mexico.[53]

The Little Tycoon was well-received, and the amateurs seemed to have reached the heights of acting, comic performance, and singing. The *Optic* reviewer's praise of individual stars sometimes included a nod to their professional lives and duties. Professor Hand, business man and musical instructor, was lauded "for the manner in which he has carried out the work . . . ;" Ned Gross, "instead of being book-keeper in a big mercantile establishment, should be the comedian of a first-class company;" and Harriet Knickerbocker, an instructor at Hand's Music School, "ranks with the best singers of America."[54]

Seven months later, on Wednesday evening, November 12th, "a large and select audience assembled at Tamme opera house . . . to do honor to the Mikado as rendered by the Las Vegas opera company . . . ." The Company's first performance of *The Mikado* (1885), an operetta by W. S. Gilbert (1836–1911) and Arthur Sullivan (1842–1900),[55] was said to be "equal to the efforts of many traveling companies which rank high as professionals." The anonymous reviewer noted the "fine stage setting and the elegance of the costumes" and went into great detail describing several of the women's gowns. Indeed, the title of the article says it all: "The Mikado. Beautiful Girls, Elegant Costumes, Fine Singing, Accomplished Acting, Good Audience."[56]

Two years later, in June of 1892, the Opera Company performed another Gilbert and Sullivan classic, *H. M. S. Pinafore* (1878). According to the review in the *Optic*, "as is usually the case, when a home talent appears before the public of Las Vegas, the opera house . . . was crowded with a sympathetic and appreciative assembly of the best people." The reviewer attributed this community support to the fact that the "home companies never fail to present something worthy of patronage." The reporter went on to praise the play "for its comicality . . . and the delightfully charming character of its airs . . . ," noting that Professor Hand trained the performers and conducted the orchestra, Edith Rothgeb accompanied on the violin, and Professor Smith drilled the cadets.

> The car drill was one of the most attractive and well-executed spectacular events ever put upon a Las Vegas stage. The movements of the young ladies were executed with the precision of a West Point cadet corps, and with the grace and rythmn [sic.] of motion usually attributed to fairies.[57]

In the same edition of the *Optic,* a letter to the editor signed "Looked On" noted that if Maude Keller and L. R. Allen had bigger parts, "the company would then be more highly appreciated, as they [the actors' roles] would be much more artistically rendered." The letter concluded with "the company should put its talents to the front."[58] Apparently, the old saying applies—everyone's a critic.

This production of *Pinafore* was especially problematic. Advertisements for *H. M. S. Pinafore* stated that it would be performed on Thursday, June 9;[59] however, late on that very afternoon, two fires broke out in separate locations of the East Las Vegas business district. The initial fire began behind J. H. Stearns' Grocery on the southwest corner of Sixth Street and Douglas Avenue, across from the Opera House.[60] Then "the Elite saloon, west of the Optic block was in deadly danger every moment, and had it caught, . . . the opera house. . . and the entire square, on sixth street . . . could not have been saved."[61] Although scheduled to perform that night, a review of *Pinafore* did not appear until June 11th and referred to a performance on June 10. The June 10th edition of the *Optic* ran an advertisement for *Pinafore,* with "elegant costumes and catchy music," stating that it would play "To-Night." It seems that the performance was wisely postponed due to the fire yet received accolades and a generous audience on opening night.[62]

Although performing and socializing were its major activities, the Las Vegas Opera Company also provided fundraising and support to local music students. Company members assisted in student recitals for Hand's Music School and participated in performances for The Hand Concert Company. On August 4, 1887, the Company gave a benefit performance of *Billee Taylor* for Dan Roads,[63] and on April 12, 1890, the group presented *The Little Tycoon,* which was glowingly reviewed, to raise funds for the "Hook and Ladder Company."[64] Several Music School events between 1890 and 1893 list Opera Company members: the Misses Rothgeb, Harriet Knickerbocker, and Max Nordhaus. One program was titled "Seventh Recital . . . Hand's

Music School Assisted by the Las Vegas Opera Company."[65] Because Harriet Knickerbocker was a faculty member at the school, she would be involved as part of her responsibilities, but other members of the Opera Company provided their services as well. There is no doubt that such assistance, from veteran, albeit amateur, performers was invaluable to the students.

❧

In the early 1890s, Las Vegans welcomed a new theatrical director and veteran actor when Alexander Randolph, originally from Scotland, abandoned a promising career in Chicago, IL, and traveled to New Mexico in an attempt to cure his tuberculosis. Randolph assembled a troupe of local amateurs under the name The Las Vegas Comedy Company, which does not seem to have any connections to the Comedy Company of 1885, and turned out three theatrical productions in quick succession.

On February 16, 1894, the Company presented *Our Boys,* "a chaste and delightfully enjoyable performance," to a large audience at the Tamme Opera House in spite of inclement weather and the Lenten season.[66] *Our Boys* (1875), written by Henry James Byron (1834–1884), is a comedy about British mores and inheritance issues. From 1875 to 1879, it had been the longest running play in London.[67]

Barely two months later, on April 6, the Company presented *Between the Acts* at the Tamme Opera House.[68] The performance garnered an "appreciative audience," and at intermission Mrs. Douglas sang and Cora Pettijohn whistled.[69]

On August 24 of the same year, Randolph and his "home artists" performed *The Ticket-of-Leave Man* (1863) by Tom Taylor (1817–1880), who suffers the distinction of having written *Our American Cousin*, the play President Abraham Lincoln was attending when he was assassinated. *The Ticket-of-Leave Man,* a melodrama about a parolee's struggle to reenter society, is the earliest known play about the seamy side of London. Its message is stated clearly by idealizing the love of a faithful woman. The play also includes one of the first appearances of a detective as an on-stage character.[70]

The *Optic* reviewer called the performance, "the finest production ever offered in this city. The characters were well-drawn, the representations natural," and Randolph is "one of the ablest actors in America." The review heaped praise upon the play as well as the Company: "The play was a strong one and strongly presented, and everyone realized that the company had passed through the hands of a master." The writer also noted that Randolph was a "quiet gentleman," who must be "proud of his profession and his ability to train amateurs."[71] Although the *Optic* had been a long-time supporter of amateur theatricals, this writer was impressed not only with the production and the play but also with the gentleman behind it.

However, what was a welcome and promising addition to the community's entertainment offerings came to a sudden and tragic halt. In the summer of 1895, Randolph shattered his thigh when he was thrown from a burro, "since which untoward event he has been confined to his bed, greatly to the damage of his feeble health." In addition to worsening his condition, the injury stole his livelihood. Randolph, "a victim of consumption," was supporting himself and his family by "giving entertainments, assisted by home talent."[72]

Both the *Optic* and the Comedy Company members came to the aid of Randolph and his family. The newspaper provided a direct appeal to the community, noting that due to the help of friends, "the family have, perhaps, not actually suffered for food" but with winter approaching, the needs would surely increase. It seemed prudent, therefore, to raise funds to send Randolph's family to Chicago to stay with relatives while he convalesced at 'the ladies' Home,' which no doubt will greatly advance" his recovery."[73] The "ladies' Home" refers to the Ladies' Relief Society, established in 1884 to "help care for the sick and destitute."[74] It later became the first Las Vegas Hospital, whose Medical Director, was Dr. Alice Rice.[74]

Randolph's Comedy Company rose to the occasion with a benefit performance. With the aid of the *Optic,* the Company set about making its plans. "Such being the condition of the case, *The Optic* feels justified in asking and the home dramatic company in expecting a most liberal patronage."[75] And on November 11, 1895,

> The Randolph comedy company covered itself with glory, last evening, in the production of "Little Lord Fauntleroy," for the benefit of Prof. Alex. Randolph. The play is a well-known and deservedly popular one, and each actor seemed admirably suited to the part he performed.[76]

The play, adapted by Frances Hodgson Burnett (1849–1924) from her novel by the same name and copyrighted in 1889, was indeed popular; however, it was also notorious, involving Burnett, Samuel French & Sons, and Frank W. Sanger, among others, in a long, drawn-out lawsuit concerning performance rights.[77]

For the Las Vegas performance, Professor Hand's orchestra played during intermission, and Professor Brannon, accompanied by Professor Miller on the piano, performed a violin solo that "was highly appreciated by all lovers of music." Members of the cast included Miss Myra Harkness as the American adventuress, Ed C. York playing the Earl of Dorincourt, and Little Maggie Burks, "whose acting is a marvel for one of her age." The performance was financially successful, "as well as otherwise, clearing above expenses in the neighborhood of $80."[78]

The members of the Las Vegas Comedy Company not only performed well together but also formed close social ties and feelings of responsibility toward one another. Additionally, the extent to which local musicians Hand, Miller, and Brannon were involved illustrates a network of support among "local talent." Because of these efforts, by 1900, Alexander Randolph and his family had been reunited and were living in Illinois with his wife's parents,[79] but Las Vegas had lost one of its up-and-coming amateur troupes.

The Baca Family Troupe, the Las Vegas Opera Company, and Randolph's Las Vegas Comedy Company illustrate the wide variety of amateur offerings in and around Las Vegas during approximately the same time period. While the Baca Troupe concentrated on secular and non-secular folk-dramas and made a name for itself throughout the Territory, the Opera Company produced flamboyantly opulent performances, provided a business and social network for its members, and supported local fundraising needs and music students. The Comedy Company rounded out the area's entertainment offerings by adding quality melodramas and solid performances to the mix. The Comedy Company also illustrates the extent of personal relationships and loyalty developed among the members of amateur performing groups as well as the continued influence of immigrants to the country and the Territory.

Soldiers relaxing at Fort Union. Photographer unknown,
Courtesy City of Las Vegas Museum and Rough Rider Memorial Collection, 2009.27.42.

3

Drama at the Fort

1883–1886

Owing to the want of any kind of amusement in this post other
than the daily playing of the Band, a few enterprising young
men of the garrison, have formed what is termed,
"The Fort Union Dramatic Society."
—Gus

ocated approximately 26 miles north of the Las Vegas settlement, Fort Union was established in 1851 to protect travelers, commercial enterprises, and outlying settlements from Kiowa and Comanche raids.[1] By the 1860s this "Guardian of the Santa Fe Trail"[2] was a bustling community of soldiers, families, civilian artisans, day laborers, and tradesmen. But when the American Civil War and the Indian Wars ended and New Mexico Territory was operating under its own governing body, the need for military protection diminished, and in 1879, the Atchison, Topeka, and Santa Fe Railroad usurped the Santa Fe Trail as the main trade route, reducing the need for escort troops and eliminating the Fort's role as supply depot. As Robert M. Utley describes the situation, "after 1879 the great freight wagons ceased to creep across the rutted plains to Fort Union, and military freight now arrived at Watrous in railroad boxcars."[3]

By the 1880s, Fort Union had became a community in want of entertainment. The garrison was bursting with bored soldiers whose work was largely ceremonial,[4] so the enlisted men rallied to the cause, organizing social clubs, a debating society, and groups devoted to intellectual pursuits.[5] In *Fort Union (New Mexico),* F. Stanley mentions such activities as holiday dinners featuring "luxuries of the East [United States]," occasional "square heel-and-toe" walking matches, and "hops" or dances: "Nothing now offers the soldier more joy than when he is carried away by the excitement of the dance."[6]

Theatrical productions were a large part of these efforts but sometimes led to controversy and charges of favoritism. Between 1883 and 1886, Fort Union supported four separate amateur acting companies, made up of enlisted men. Based on newspaper accounts, many of the Fort's amateur offerings followed the minstrel show format. An evening's entertainment often included songs and dancing; short comic sketches and impersonations; jokes and exhibitions such as contortion acts, Indian club-swinging, and bone solos. Usually sketches and plays, either dramatized or in tableaux style, were presented as finales. As in Las Vegas, amateur productions at Fort Union were often associated with raising funds. Additional issues that arose at the garrison included concerns about the decency of the theatrical content, attendance and support from officers, and favoritism in the ranks. Some companies enjoyed more attention than others, and one, the Fort Union Dramatic Society, became the basis of a feud between two regimental correspondents which played out in the pages of the *Las Vegas Gazette* and *Daily Optic.*

In the spring of 1883, in response to boredom and a lack of entertainment at the post, a group of soldiers formed the Fort Union Dramatic Society. According to Gus, the regimental correspondent to the *Optic,* the purpose of the Society was "to give, every now and then, an entertainment which will serve to enliven the otherwise monotonous life of the soldier whilst in the garrison." Gus noted that with hard work and the support of the garrison officers, the founding group of twelve men would soon "give the post a few good enjoyable evenings."[7]

By October of the same year, two theatrical companies were producing "a few good enjoyable evenings." In his *Optic* column of October 9, 1883, Gus previewed upcoming productions of the Dramatic Society and another troupe, the Fort Union Comedy Company. He reported that the Comedy Company would be performing at the garrison on October 11th, a Wednesday evening, and that "the dramatic society are busy as bees preparing to go to your city [Las Vegas] and give a performance on the 17th and 18th . . . ."[8]

However, Gus did not seem to have much confidence in the Comedy Company when he wrote that their presentation "is expected to be something good. We shall hope so at least." He went into more detail about the Dramatic Society: "the program for the 17th has been shown your correspondent and it is indeed a creditable one," and he assured his readers that the Dramatic Society was "as good, if not better than most professional traveling shows. In it [the Society] they have talent and wit." According to Gus, the members of this group were "well educated and perfect gentlemen."[9]

The Comedy Company did indeed perform on October 11, 1883, at the post opera house,[10] presenting an evening of variety acts and skits. In his column of October 16, Gus reviewed the production as "a very amusing entertainment" and described the activities. The evening's offerings included songs, "jokes and other funny sayings," farces, and a number of comic skits. Gus praised the singing performances, noting that they "showed quite an improvement." The finale, "Skidmore Guards," was a favorite: "It took down the house and received a perfect storm of applause," but for Gus, a soldier named Flannery was the star:

His specialty act, "The Regular Army," was the most laughable feature of the evening's performance. Flannery is a natural born comedian. He deserves great success for his efforts in this entertainment, for he is the very life and soul of the comedy company.

The performance was a financial success as well, "the house was pretty well crowded," and Gus declared that the group's performance had "improved greatly since its last appearance." He closed the review with a hope to see them appear again soon and a comment on the company's costuming: "Their uniform in the first part was very pretty and neatly made up."[11] It seems that the Company lived up to its name by focusing on laughter. "Skidmore Guards" and "The Regular Army" were interpretations of the contemporary songs and skits of Edward Harrigan (1844–1911) and Tony Hart (1855–91), which, through comedy, depicted "the lives and struggles" of Irish immigrants and African-Americans in the military.[12]

While the Comedy Company was making a big hit with variety acts and comic skits, the Dramatic Society was deep in preparations for taking its show on the road. Gus noted that the Society had completed arrangements to perform with the post band in Las Vegas, and he praised the Society in general: "The dramatic society gives a remarkably good show for amateurs." Gus also pointed out that the Las Vegas performance was a fundraiser for the post school, a "noble object."[13]

On October 17th, an advertisement in the *Optic* announced that the "Ft Union Dramatic Club [sic.] assisted by the 23rd Infantry Band" would present a "Grand Dramatic and Music Entertainment" at the "OPERA HOUSE." As mentioned earlier, the famous Tamme, later Duncan, Opera House was not opened until 1886; therefore, the advertisement is referring to the Ward and Tamme Opera House on Railroad Avenue. Tickets for this performance were advertised at 50 cents for a single and 75 cents for reserved seats. The advertisement included an appeal for attendance: "It is for the benefit of little children whose parents are soldiers, and who have no educational advantages whatever."[14]

On opening night, October 17, it seemed the appeal was successful. An unsigned *Optic* review entitled "Last Night's Entertainment" stated that the "inspiring strains of the 23rd Infantry band drew a crowd of people to the opera house last night, and by eight o'clock, the auditorium was comfortably filled, while nearly every reserved seat was occupied."[15] The production opened with a musical selection, "Lucretia Borgia," performed by Professors Miller, Berninger, and Erdman followed by the sketches, "Paddy Mile's Boy" with John T. Smith as "Patty's [sic.] bad boy" and "The Haunted House" with Joseph Kemp in the lead. Next came more songs, dances, speeches, Indian club swinging by C. Conley, and J. Massier's contortion act. The climax of the evening was a play, *The Irish Attorney of Ireland, 1770,* in which Shaw and Murphy played the leads. "A pleasant dance to first-rate music" topped off the evening.[16] Reviews of individual performances were glowing:

> "The Haunted House" showed a good bit of eccentric negro impersonation by Joseph Kemp, and W. L. Beyer showed splendid facial expression and good acting as Mrs. Fidget. Murphy's rattling character song, 'Long Barney' was a life-like interpretation of Irish ways.[17]

According to *Fort Union (New Mexico)*, by F. Stanley, the Dramatic Society was a "First Class organization." Its members were talented and "would be entitled to a place on the legitimate stage. Constant practice and rehearsal has made a notable absence of breaks and delays so common in amateur performers."[18] Given such praise, most likely the group anticipated a successful engagement; however, although the production was well received, poor attendance for the second performance resulted in a disappointing financial outcome.[19] An *Optic* reviewer stated that the group had "labored under several disadvantages," pointing out that the Society's performance "followed close on the heels of a professional minstrel troupe who took all the spare cash from amusement lovers." Furthermore, it seemed that most of the theatre-going "population of the city was saddened by the sorrowful accident a Los Alamos lake."[20] Los Alamos, not the atomic city, was an agricultural settlement of 24 families about eleven miles north of Las Vegas.[21]

The second night's performance, a condensed version of the first, also included a grand ball.[22] At the close of the performance portion, John T. Smith, "Patty's bad boy," came onstage and thanked the audience and the town for their support. According to the newspaper item, William F. Granlee was the company's production manager.[23]

Gus, however, minimized the financial disappointment and focused on how well the Society was received. "Financially their performances were not as successful as was anticipated, nevertheless the reception . . . was extremely gratifying." Gus also noted that the expenses associated with transporting the band reduced the profits. He reported that "The boys express themselves well repaid for their trouble by the courteous treatment" they received, and they thanked the *Optic* and the *Gazette* for "the many favors done them in the shape of kindly notices and criticisms."[24]

At this time, there was some general concern about the potentially offensive content of theatrical productions and the responses of the audiences. In his preview of the Dramatic Society's offerings, Gus had stressed the absence of vulgarity or indecency. "All their plays are modest and respectable. They have always rejected dramas that deviate in the slightest degree from decency," and their "performances here [Fort Union] have been marked for the absence of anything vulgar."[25] Because on any given night in Las Vegas, the audience might include bandits, railroad crews, and cowboys and because recent amusements, such as "'The Female Bathers,'"[26] had drawn large, vocal audiences, Gus' remarks may be a warranted attempt to discourage the more boisterous attendees.

For Gus, the new year began with a ray of hope for the improved quality of the Fort's amateur productions. He wrote that on January 12, 1884, the Dramatic Society presented "one of the most interesting entertainments ever seen at this post."

It was distinctly a dramatic entertainment and was entirely different from any other performance given at the Fort Union opera house. The dramatic society saw the propriety of giving an entertainment somewhat above the farces and sketches which were most generally presented.[27]

Considering the severity of Northern New Mexico winters, it must have been "most interesting" because on this occasion, the Fort Union Opera House "was filled to the utmost capacity," and many audience members had traveled significant distances to attend. In spite of the biting cold of January and the distances, some as far as 30 miles, from their respective locations, theatrical patrons such as "Mr. Edward Friend of the Las Vegas Optic; Mr. Alvey of the Mora County Pioneer; Miss Dunlap of Las Vegas; [and] Mr. Campbell of Watrous"[28] made the journey. Although rail service was available from Las Vegas to Watrous, visitors would then complete their journeys, about six additional miles of open prairie, by horseback, carriage, wagon, or on foot. Possibly, the garrison provided a horse-drawn shuttle.

The program began with the usual variety acts, and several individual performances stood out. There was a clog dance by William Kerwin, who "has few, if any, superiors among the noted professionals," with an encore by Kerwin's pupil, Master Willie Bolton, age 14, "who showed remarkable proficiency in the art of dancing."[29] Then Mr. Simpson, who "has a very pleasing voice," sang "There'll Be No One to Welcome Me Home," which was "well-received as a beautiful floral tribute from the hands of some 'fair one' attests."[30] It is a comment on the times and the presence of the railroad that this young lady was able to produce a "floral tribute," presumably fresh flowers, in the middle of winter.

The singing and dance performances were followed by Mr. Beyer's comic recitations which recalled "the witty and captivating 'Fritz Emmet, '"a reference to Joseph K. Emmet, a New York performer and comedian of the time.[31] Beyer's performance included "Remarks on Temperance" and "Maude Mule," a parody of "Maude Miller,"[32] a popular poem, which in 1909, became the basis of a film, *Maude Muller,* a domestic drama.[33] Next came Indian club-swinging by Mr. Conley who "possesses strength and powers of endurance seldom found in an ordinary man."[34] The variety portion concluded with a song and dance by Kerwin and Shaw that "set the audience wild with enthusiasm."[35]

However, for Gus, the highlight of the evening was the contemporary drama, *More Sinned Against Than Sinning* (1882), by John Louis Carleton (1861–?), a prolific amateur playwright of Saint John, New Brunswick. Carleton was said to be a master at providing stage directions, especially regarding blocking, tableaux, and ending scenes. The play was particularly appropriate for amateur productions and popular throughout the United States.[36]

Gus praised the drama, presented "in a prologue and three acts," as an accurate depiction of contemporary land issues in Ireland: "the pernicious system, [sic.] of leaving complete control of rented estates to land agents, who have neither conscience or honor." Gus applauded the acting, the "very neat plot," and the Dramatic Society for taking a chance on a serious presentation. However, he noted that it was "but fairly presented . . . . The chief faults lay in the neglect of the drop curtain, which left the performers in a very embarrassing predicament. . . . and a few blunders in very unseasonable places . . . ." In spite of these inconveniences, it was a "brilliant performance," and Gus stated that the audience considered the evening a success. The proceeds went to the Fort Union School.[37]

Gus expressed high hopes for the future of such entertainments and for continuing improvements in the Society's presentations. He stated that *More Sinned Against than Sinning* was a "venture," and that the Society members had been uncertain as to the outcome. They were pleasantly surprised when "the drama was appreciated in a manner which was highly flattering to the performers, and which filled them with courage and bright hopes for the future."[38] In a later correspondence, April 29, it becomes clear that Gus, at some time, was a member of the Society and may have been involved in this production.

Despite his high hopes, Gus's next mention of the theatrical scene does not bode well for improvements. By February, both acting companies were experiencing difficulties: "the comedy company is a thing of the past, and the dramatic society have [sic.] taken a very much needed vacation." Gus also pointed out that the theatrical productions of both troupes had been "well patronized," and he encouraged them to reorganize: "Come, boys, do something in the shape of a performance."[39]

By the following month, things had not improved much although the Comedy Company did resurface. Gus wrote, "just now we are suffering for the want of amusement of any kind," but he included a report on the Saint Patrick's Day celebration. The "comedy company headed by the grand marshal of the day, Serg't Patrick Harm," led a gala parade which started from the Comedy Company headquarters and included a delegation from each military company "in full regalia," the 23rd Infantry band, civilian employees, and the "water wagon drawn by eight mules" and decorated in green with "Irish emblems such as the harp and the shamrock." The long procession marched through the garrison several times, and later everyone partook in "a merry dance till early dawn."[40]

On April 14, 1884, the Dramatic Society made its come-back with a "select variety entertainment;"[41] however, this production became the catalyst for a vitriolic discourse between two Fort Union correspondents, known only as "Gus" and "Jud," over issues related to the quality of theatrical productions and nepotism in the military. This public altercation illustrates the extent to which loyalties, combined with questionable military practices, affected performances, players, audiences, and critics. The roots of the argument can be traced to one of the Society's earlier productions. Unfortunately, the only surviving documents related to this feud are Gus's *Optic* columns, "Our Fort Union Letter," and his rebuttal to Jud's accusations.

For Gus, the April 14th production did not fulfill those "bright hopes" of January. The company presented another evening of skits, songs, parlor gymnastics, a bone solo, a clog dance, and the two-act drama, *The End of His Tether*. Although it played to the largest audience yet, Gus wrote: "The cast of the drama was weak. The drama itself was a dry one and unless the cast is excellent, it will ever be a failure." However, Gus gave credit where he saw credit due. He praised the performance of Miss Nellie Day, who did "very well, taking everything into consideration;" Billy Adams, who "made the most favorable impressions of any actor who has appeared before a Fort Union audience;" Joe Kemp's "Ethiopian eccentricities;" and Mr. Vanderhoef, Master Willie Bolton, W. L. Beyer, and John Bryan.

At the same time, Gus pointed out that "the acting of some characters would not stand the test."

> We must say that those who in vain have have [sic.] endeavored to become actors, and have failed just as often as they have attempted, we must say that they should take a back seat and cry "enough."

Although in general he praised the performance of Billy Adams, Gus did not hesitate to point out that Adams "did not properly interpret his part," but rather, "departed widely from the character." Gus noted that some members of the Dramatic Society were talented but that "there are some who should not appear before an audience." Overall, Gus judged the cast members to be inadequate, "the general performance of the drama could not be called good," but admitted that it was "no worse than the usual performance of this society" and noted the attendance of the commanding officer, Colonel Black.[42]

Apparently, Gus's critique garnered an attack from someone else at the Fort who wrote a rebuttal for the *Gazette,* April 26, 1884, and signed himself "Jud." Within days, Gus took up the gauntlet. In his April 29th *Optic* correspondence, subtitled "Gus Goes for 'Jud', a Gazette Correspondent, Who has the Boldness to Style Himself an Actor," Gus questioned the identity and the character of his opponent, referring to Jud as "a party, or rather parties, in this post, in which your correspondent [Gus] received a rather severe rubbing," and he dubbed Jud "Mrs Judy Hangeron."[43]

In defending himself, Gus indicated that in his April 17th critique he was attempting to concentrate on what he saw as the main focus of theatrical productions—talent. Gus then indicted the entire group that Jud represented: "there is neither talent nor manliness in the whole gang." Gus claimed that Jud and his cronies could not accept Gus's account of the evening because it "did not satisfy the vain, ignorant, green fakes who have the boldness and hayseed effrontery to make an attempt at acting." Gus countered Jud's accusation of an "unjust and contradictory" review by stating that Jud did not prove his claim. Then Gus attacked Jud personally:

> . . . you are foolish, you are vain, and "Jud," you are a snide actor. You have lent yourself to throw the balls others moulded [sic.] but dare not use. You may be petted, perhaps recommended for promotion for your dirty ways . . . . You are not long enough in the service to know any better than to curry favor, but you are old enough to know that by such work you shall earn for yourself the unenvied title of 'sucker.'[44]

Gus continued with a warning that Jud had "championed the wrong crowd to the expense of one who is your superior, and theirs, mentally, physically and morally," apparently referring to Gus, himself. Then Gus provided a second criticism of "The End of His Tether" focusing on Mr. Granlee, who "became completely muddled in his part," Mr. Heintze who continually dropped his lines, and Mr. Adams who departed as far as he could from the role of The Inventor "without completely losing sight" of the character.

In concluding his rebuttal, Gus revealed that this altercation had a history. He referred to the Dramatic Society's earlier production "in Las Vegas, some months ago" when Gus was a member of the organization. According to Gus, the people he criticized, including

Jud, were the cause of the troupe's return, "disgraced," from that engagement stating that even after "many and many rehearsals these parties went before the public and made blunder after blunder, forgot line after line, and still they have the boldness to appear again." Gus emphasized that whenever the Dramatic Society performed, "they [sic.] made complete dupes of themselves and all who had the misfortune to appear with them." Clearly, this battle had been brewing for sometime because the only reference to a Dramatic Society performance in Las Vegas is to the one that took place on October 17 and 18, 1883.

Gus ended with:

> The talent of the dramatic society consists of Messers. Adams, Beyer, Kemp and Vanderhoef. Jud, take the rest and place them in the police cart and dump 'em into the nearest refuse heap and then place yourself on the top of the heap as a monument to ignorance and stupidity.[45]

Little more than a week later, the *Optic* reported that the 23rd Infantry regiment had been transferred to Michigan taking Gus with it:

> "Gus," our faithful correspondent, has been very valuable to us and has made quite an interesting feature for The Optic in this post. His writings have demonstrated that he is a man of few prejudices and much general information. We dislike to say good bye . . . .

The article ended with the statement that the *Optic* intended to make Gus its "regular authorized correspondent to the east."[46]

The feud between Gus and Jud reveals several agendas among some of the amateur actors at Fort Union. It is clear that Gus was involved in the Dramatic Society's production in Las Vegas and that some of the actors in the troupe dropped the ball leaving other actors, perhaps Gus himself, high and dry or rather upstaged. In addition,

Gus's counter-attack on Jud infers the existence of favoritism. Gus's vitriolic reply, although directed at Jud, sent messages to other enlisted men as well as officers. Gus referred to Jud as a "sucker and an ignorant dupe," and he told Jud, "you may be petted, perhaps recommended for promotion for your dirty ways, but then you can never be a man."[47] Gus assumed, and perhaps rightly so, that Jud had written in defense of the actors in question merely to further his own ambitions. And finally, in his discussion of *More Sinned Against Than Sinning,* Gus showed a deep concern regarding the quality of the productions, individual performances, and the plays at the post.

According to F. Stanley, Gus was always writing. It was rumored that "he wrote a novel at Fort Union . . . [and] successful plays for Broadway . . . ." However, Stanley did not corroborate this information or further identify Gus.[48] Gus was a member of the 23rd Infantry, and in his column about Saint Patrick's Day, he identified himself as Irish. Giese's graduate thesis, *Social Life at Fort Union, New Mexico in the 1880s*, points out that sometimes the garrison writers engaged in disagreements, criticisms, and "lengthy battles between correspondents of different regiments."

Whatever the causes may have been, the feud had a ripple effect. By May of 1884, the Fort Union Comedy Company reorganized as the Fort Union Minstrel Troupe and made its first appearance "in the Fort Union Opera House." Directed by Mr. Hauch, the program included three skits, songs by Haggery, Shaw, and McAuliffe, and several comic sketches. According to Giese, "Skidmore Guards," previously performed in October of 1883, "the entire company dressed in fancy military uniforms" and led by Ed Mongus, marched and sang "The Skids are out today."[49] Jon Finson's study of minstrelsy references a song, "The Skidmore Guard" (1874), music by David Braham (1838–1905) and lyrics by Edward "Ned" Harrigan (1844–1911), and Finson suggests that "The Skidmore Guard" was the Black counterpart of "The Mulligan Guard," which was a popular parody of a "uniformed shooting club" performed by Harrigan and Hart.[50]

Another sketch that evening, "High Jack, the Heeler," was

presented "without breaks or pauses," and a burlesque quartet sang "Bad Whiskey." A skit entitled "Mr. and Mrs. Malone" brought down the house with "deafening applause and several curtain calls." The evening concluded with a performance of "Serenade." Professor Berringer's full orchestra provided the music, which was said to be "far superior to the Fort Union Dramatic Society's 'lame fiddle and organ.'"[51]

In June of 1885, the "G. W." minstrels offered "two entertainments." Although the group drew favorable audiences at each performance, a garrison correspondent signing himself "Critic" chastised the post officers for a lack of support for the organization's efforts. The reviewer stated that the presence of the officers would encourage the "considerable talent lying dormant," and thus Fort Union "could soon boast of having the finest organization of the kind in the territory."[52] Ironically, "Critic" offered no critical analysis of the performances.

Perhaps inspired by such calls to action, "a young author whose sphere of life should be outside of the army," wrote "Ben Bolt," a melo-drama, possibly fashioned after the 1842 ballad of the same title by Thomas Dunn and set to music by Nelson Kneass in 1848.[53] On October 26th, the Dramatic Society performed "Ben Bolt" at the "opera house." Mars, another regimental correspondent to the *Optic,* did not identify the playwright by name and noted that the play would "hardly pass before a critical audience." However, he went on to say that it was "good enough for this post and was well received" with "standing room unobtainable long before the curtain rose." Mars declined to provide a critique because the actors were amateurs and "need a great deal more experience before they come within the pale of criticism."[54]

However, in the same correspondence, Mars did not hesitate to criticize a "tenor singer of the minstrel troupe here" whom he applauded for resigning "per request." But Mars warned the Las Vegas public that this singer would be taking up the writing life with a "correspondence for certain papers." Mars also inferred that the singer was a drunkard: "Agua pura, applied in large quantities to the debris of his brain, might stimulate its action . . . ." Earlier in the same correspondence, Mars described the difficulties of writers to publish with large magazines and publishing houses and praised the "country newspaper" as a rich field for writers to plough. Mars ended with a tidbit of theatre gossip. At the close of the theatrical production, "a 'crooked' soldier was prowling around the kitchens on the officers' line" and "frightened some of the girls."[55]

In "Fort Union Item," February 17, 1886, an anonymous reporter stated that the Acme Comedy Company would soon "give their patrons a treat . . . . A lively comedy from the pen of H. C. Byron [sic.] author of 'Orpheus Eurydice,' 'Our Boys,' 'The Girls,' 'Weak Woman' etc, is in rehearsal."[56] The brief article about the Acme Comedy Company noted that rehearsals were in progress at the Fort, so this would be another group of amateur soldier-performers. According to Giese, the Acme Comedy Company made its debut at the garrison with a production entitled "Uncle," which "the boys warmly received."[57]

Although Gus and other correspondents attested to the constant ennui and isolation at Fort Union, a snapshot of the amateur theatrics of the mid-1880s indicates otherwise. There were not only several active performing groups but also fierce loyalties, heated feuds about the qualities of the productions, and dynamic relationships among performers. Regardless of the true extent of their influences, amateur thespians brought contemporary entertainment and civilian audience members to the garrison thereby relieving some of the boredom.

Music Festival

"The Creation"

Las Vegas &&
Oratorio Society

Duncan Opera House >>
Las Vegas, New Mexico
Wednesday and Thursday
June 21-22, 1899 >>

PRESS OF LAS VEGAS PUBLISHING CO.

Program cover from the first Las Vegas performance of "The Creation."
Press of Las Vegas, Courtesy City of Las Vegas Museum and Rough Rider
Memorial Collection, 2006.24.6.

Epilogue

The Close of a Century, 1899

As the twentieth century advanced, amateur productions found themselves in competition with college performing arts programs, the fledgling film industry, and traveling extravaganzas like Pawnee Bill's Wild West Shows. The New Mexico Normal School offered music and drama programs. Motion picture production companies like those of Romaine Fielding and Tom Mix discovered the location amenities of Las Vegas and its open country. The 1890s saw some local performance halls and opera houses abandoned or converted to alternative uses. In 1897, the mighty Tamme Opera House on Douglas Avenue, where many of the amateur performances had taken place, changed ownership and was renamed the Duncan Opera House. Throughout the ensuing twelve years, Opera House management changed eight times, and by 1922, the K & F Amusement Company was maintaining it "for road shows."[1]

However, such setbacks did not hinder the local talent spirit. In November of 1898, a new and ambitious group organized a company that would combine the talents of local amateurs with the experience and skills of professionals. The Las Vegas Oratorio Society formed for the purpose of providing musical entertainment for the Territorial Educational Convention held in Las Vegas "during the holidays" of 1898, and on June 21 and 22, 1899, the Oratorio Society presented a Music Festival featuring Josef Hayden's oratorio, "The Creation," at the Duncan Opera House. Under the direction of James Graham McNary, this production brought soloists from Saint Louis and Chicago; however, the lead soprano was Las Vegas's own Harriet Knickerbocker, the accompanists, Elisabeth Cooley and Ruth Raynolds, also were home grown talent, and local musician and conductor, Max Norhaus, participated in the performance. Additionally, the names of several Opera Company performers—Rothgeb, Hofmiester, and Wean, appeared in the program.[2]

The Oratorio Society differed from other Las Vegas amateur groups in that its productions were oratorios, that is, dramatic musical programs consisting of arias, recitations, duets, and choruses. By its nature, the Oratorio Society provided a vehicle for the area's music and drama students as well as long-time amateur performers. Indicative of the times, the productions were lavish and on a grand scale. The 1899 Music Festival featured four soloists, two accompanists, and a large chorus.[3]

The great chorus of seventy voices filled the entire stage and presented a most charming scene. Among its members were seen many of the most prominent ladies, and business and professional men of Las Vegas.[4]

Homer Moore, a well-known baritone and musician, provided the *Optic* with a review, and a representative of the newspaper interviewed one of the program soloists, Milton B. Griffith, Tenor. Griffith had been McNary's professor and fellow performer with the Tarkio College quartet in Missouri.[5] The comprehensive review glowingly described Las Vegas, its "handsome homes, whole souled people," and hospitality in addition to its excellent musical talent.

Both Griffith and Moore praised the musical director:

> Mr. McNary, for a young man of his age certainly shows remarkable talent for handling a large body of singers. His ability in this direction is indicated by the unlimited confidence of the people and harmonious working of the chorus . . . . His musical instinct and keen appreciation of the artistic are quite marked . . . .[6]

At the time, McNary was a new faculty member at New Mexico Normal University,[7] which would later become New Mexico Highlands University. He spent several years in Las Vegas and married Ruth Raynolds, one of the accompanists for "The Creation" and the daughter of local banker Joshua S. Raynolds.[8] A few years later, when McNary was editor of the *Optic,* he ended up in a street brawl with the editor of a rival newspaper, Earl Lyons, and towards the end of his stay in Las Vegas, McNary served as New Mexico Territory's "public printer, conceived of and published *The Optic Cartoon Book* and purchased an interest in the Optic Publishing Company."[9]

The chorus and the accompanists also received warm praise: "The vocal talent in the chorus is far above the average and there is a beauty of tone quality that one rarely hears." Regarding the accompanists, Griffith explained their importance to a successful program and stated that he found "Misses Cooley and Raynolds two accomplished pianists who can accompany any singer. There is quite an art in accompanying." However, the star of the evening was Harriet Knickerbocker, who was proclaimed "The Leading Soprano of the Southwest."[10]

At this point in her career, Knickerbocker was an accomplished vocalist. In addition to soloist for the Music Festival, she was a founding member and performed regularly with the Las Vegas Opera Company, she taught at Hand's Music School, performed with the Hand Concert Company of Las Vegas,[11] and on January 14, she opened the 1892–93 season at the Ellis Club of Los Angeles, California.[12] In 1888, after hearing Knickerbocker sing at "the West Side Catholic

Church," L. Von Meyerhoff arranged for her to perform at the Phoenix Hotel in Montezuma, New Mexico, at his *"Tafalmûjik* (table-music)" performances:

> Therefore you are herewith respectfully solicited by the management of the Phoenix to charm, elevate and delight the guests . . . , thus fulfilling your glorious mission as a singer by way of making happy an appreciative audience with the gift that God has blessed you with [sic.].[13]

In the *Optic* article, Moore noted that oratorio "is a high plane of musical art to which few attain," and he stated that Knickerbocker

> . . . has a splendid—a magnificent voice—a voice which has the sure foundation for making even a much greater artist, and I believe has qualities that with thorough cultivation, would make her one of the first singers in the musical world.[14]

1899 stretched Las Vegas's audiences and amateurs in several directions. A few days after the Oratorio Society's production, the First Volunteer Cavalry veterans, popularly known as Roosevelt's Rough Riders, converged on Las Vegas for their first reunion since the Spanish-American War. Colonel Theodore Roosevelt, the officers of the regiment, and its "Gallant Troopers" took part in the activities which included an encampment at Lincoln Park, memorial services for the fallen, regimental reviews and receptions, pyrotechnics, games, parades, concerts, and a ball at the Montezuma Hotel. On June 25, 1899, the Oratorio Society provided a repeat performance of "The Creation" at the Duncan Opera House[15] "for the exclusive entertainment of the Rough Riders, who filled the building." Colonel Roosevelt "stayed through to the end and was highly complimentary."[16] Another of Las Vegas's amateur performers, Louis Hofmeister, served as President of the Music Committee for the Reunion citizens' program.[17]

Later that year, on November 6, Las Vegas welcomed a new

amateur group, when the Meadow City Minstrels presented a show at the Duncan Opera House to benefit the local fire departments.[18] Two familiar names appear in the program—Pearl Wean and Maggie Burks. Although it received little newspaper coverage, it is possible that this event is the "home talent play" Lynn Perrigo described as requiring the director to eject from the audience several "young men of 'the best families'" because of their rowdy behavior.[19]

Thus, at the close of the 19th century, Las Vegas's unpredictable audiences supported a large-scale and sophisticated Music Festival, at least one minstrel show, and three days of festivities associated with the Rough Riders reunion. Amateur performers accounted for a large quantity of entertainment in a community that sprang from agricultural land grants and grew to be one of the largest trading centers of New Mexico Territory. Undaunted in the face of outlaws, vigilantes, and fires, these amateurs provided their community with secular and non-secular folk dramas; minstrel, vaudeville, and burlesque shows; and drama, melodrama, operetta, and oratorio. At a time when everything arrived by wagon and then rail, these troupers managed to acquire scripts, costumes, props, and musical instruments. The actors and actresses performed in both Spanish and English. They raised funds for fire companies and needy individuals, encouraged and tutored up-and-coming performers, and they expanded Las Vegas's reputation to include that of quality, home-grown talent.

At Fort Union, the soldiers provided much-needed diversions from a garrison grown seedy with under use. As gallant on stage as on patrol, the amateur performance companies earned fierce loyalties and enjoyed welcoming audiences both at the Fort and in Las Vegas. Fort Union contributed to the financial growth of the area and, for a time, experienced its own "boom." In 1891, the Fort was decommissioned.

In the years between 1870 and 1899, Las Vegas saw major increases in population, wealth, and diversity. Its amateur performing companies rode the rising tide of prosperity and brought entertainment, camaraderie, and support as well as a touch of glamour and sophistication to "the hottest town in the country."[20]

Afterword

ecapturing the efforts of amateur performing groups in early Las Vegas and Fort Union was arduous, tedious, challenging, and compelling. Surviving documentation is contradictory, and the performers and organizers are not available for interviews. Many physical traces such as opera houses and halls are no longer standing; photographs are few and scattered; newspaper accounts, although they provide the immediacy of the performances, often make vague reference to places, players, and plays that the readers of the time understood but that make a researcher scratch her head. If costumes and sets survived, they remain hidden away in attics, unknown or unidentified.

Therefore, in order to present a sound description of my topic, I limited the study to amateur acting companies in the Las Vegas settlements and at Fort Union between the years 1871–1899. I focused on organized groups of non-professional actors and actresses who came together to produce theatrical performances. I use the term *organized* loosely because the groups, themselves, were organized loosely. I excluded college performances and concentrated on community theatre companies, that is, companies organized by and for the communities in which they performed.

Part of limiting any study demands defining terms. An *amateur* is one who engages in a pursuit as a pastime rather than as a profession, or one who lacks experience. The word *amateur* is derived from the Latin *amator* and carries the additional meanings of a devotee, an admirer, or a lover. A *troupe* is a group of theatrical performers. So this book proffers an overview of the groups, their performances, and the plays they presented to hometown audiences.

Community theatre is born of and reflects the community from which is stems. Las Vegas bookkeepers and housekeepers, laborers and craftsmen, clerks, teachers, and politicians donned costumes and makeup, transforming themselves into actors, actresses, songsters, and dancers. Sometimes the bank cashier directed the play. Sometimes the mother of young children sang a solo, and sometimes the children performed, always stealing the show. At Fort Union, soldiers lay down their rifles and sabres to take up costumes and make-up, playing both male and female roles. The amateur groups outlined in this book brought entertainment but also nurtured a sense of pride and unity. Often their productions were intended solely to enliven the frontier experience, but at other times, the plays they selected dealt with controversial issues such as domestic violence, alcoholism, and political abuses. So too, the members of these amateur companies formed strong bonds, fierce loyalties, and when needed, they provided support and comfort to one another.

From 1871 through 1899, approximately eleven local acting companies, an opera company, and an oratorio society performed in the halls and opera houses of the wild young settlement. There were Spanish-language groups producing both secular and non-secular drama, folk-drama, and comedy. The Fort Union groups concentrated on comedy and variety shows with a nod to contemporary social issues. The Las Vegas Opera Company presented popular and comic operettas, and several acting troupes offered comedies, minstrel shows, and melodrama with a message.

These dedicated, amateur companies were ambitious and diverse in their memberships and in the types of entertainment they produced. Some of the organizations held together over a period of years while others seemed to have been one-hit-wonders—forming, performing, and evolving or disbanding. The actors and actresses played to unruly frontier audiences in the local opera houses, halls, and theatres. In addition to providing entertainment, these companies enhanced the social and educational demands of a dynamic and diverse population and offered aid and support to those in need.

This edition of *Footlights in the Foothills* includes my best effort at describing the amateur performing companies in Las Vegas, East Las Vegas, Upper Las Vegas, and Fort Union from approximately 1871 to 1899. It is by no means comprehensive, for that would require volumes. In 2009, I retraced my original research steps and uncovered additional information about the plays and playwrights these amateurs sought, found, and produced. Some topics in this study, such as the Las Vegas pioneer troupe, the Baca Family Troupe, the various acting companies associated with *las socidades*, the Las Vegas Dramatic Society, and the early days at Fort Union could benefit from increased exploration. One of the things that continues to perplex me is how scripts, costumes, sets, and props were acquired. These issues I leave for the next generation of scholars interested in amateur theatricals. I am pleased to present this snapshot of amateur acting companies, their productions, and venues as well as a discussion of their significance and contributions to the communities in which they performed.

Aknowledgements

No research project is completed in a vacuum. My first expression of gratitude is reserved for Mary Jo and Joe Morgan who began The Las Vegas Community Theatre Group in 1982. Their dedication to community productions allowed me to get involved. It was hard work—memorizing lines, cues, blocking, and the nuances of timing; gathering, designing, or making costumes, sets, and props; and securing performance venues. As amateurs, we did it all. This company evolved into the Las Vegas Players and ultimately was renamed for one of its founding members. The Nat Gold Players continues to provide entertainment and enthusiastic support of the performing arts.

One of my non-acting duties for the Players was publicity, and when composing a press release, I thought it would be fun to include a tidbit about Las Vegas's previous amateur performing groups. This thought was the impetus for *Footlights in the Foothills*. My early forays into researching Las Vegas's amateur companies began with three graduate theses. I am grateful to Dorothy LeGault, Aurora Lucero-White, and Dale Frederick Giese, whose works provided me with information and leads to the area's early amateurs.

Over the years, I amassed a good bit of information resulting in the article, "Footlights in the Foothills, the Drama of Las Vegas, New Mexico." My next thank you goes to the editors and staff of *El Palacio, The Magazine of the Museum of New Mexico,* who saw fit to publish the piece in 1990. Some years later, I returned to the project, expanded the original article, and printed the chapbook, *Footlights in the Foothills, Amateur Theatre in Las Vegas, New Mexico 1871–1899.* For research assistance on the article, the chapbook, and this 2010 edition, I thank Sue Parham, formerly of Carnegie Library, Las Vegas, New Mexico; Linda Gegick at the City of Las Vegas Museum and Rough Rider Memorial Collection; Magee Nelson of the Citizens' Committee for Historic Preservation, Las Vegas, New Mexico; Claudette Norman, Valerie Duran, Tibur Reminyk, and Mario Medina of Fort Union National Monument; and the countless people who provided anonymous assistance with microfilm machines.

For careful reading of manuscripts in the several phases of *Footlights in the Foothills,* I am indebted to Patricia Barrué-Coffman, Deborah Blanche, Jane Hyatt, Robert and Mary Johnston, Roy Luján, Jillian Rael, and Katahdin Whithnall. A special thank you goes to Amanda Ruffin for design, layout, technical consulting, and general hair-pulling on the chapbook edition. I offer my sincere appreciation to Linda Gegick for technical and design help with illustrations for the Sunstone Press edition as well as her enthusiastic support of the project. At Sunstone Press, my gratitude goes to James Clois Smith for editorial and technical assistance and for believing in *Footlights in the Foothills.*

For translations, without which the rich detail of the Spanish-language performances may have been lacking, I gratefully acknowledge the help of Patricia Barrué-Coffman, Sara Harris, and Roy Luján.

To Dorothy Le Gault, I extend my sincere gratitude for her apt title.

And to anyone I may have inadvertently omitted, I send heartfelt apologies.

Notes

Prologue

1. Anselmo Arellano and Julián Josué Vigil, *Las Vegas Grandes on the Gallinas 1835–1985* (Las Vegas, New Mexico: Editorial Teleraña, 1985), 6-16.
2. Lynn Perrigo, *Gateway to Glorieta, A History of Las Vegas, New Mexico* (New Edition. Santa Fe: Sunstone Press, 2010), 1.
3. F. Stanley, *The Las Vegas (New Mexico) Story* (New Edition. Santa Fe: Sunstone Press, 2012), 109.
4. John E. Englekirk, "The Source and Dating of New Mexico Spanish Folk Plays," *Western Folklore* (October 1957): 252 n. 71.
5. J. L. Kittle, "Folk Music of the Upper Rio Grande," *Southwest Review* 30, (1945): 193.
6. Aurora Lucero-White, "*Coloquios de los pastores de Las Vegas*" (master's thesis, New Mexico Highlands University, 1932), iv.
7. Lucero-White, "*Coloquios*," iv-v.
8. Lucero-White, "*Coloquios*," v-vi.
9. Lucero-White, "*Coloquios*," vi-vii.
10. Englekirk, "Source and Dating," 235.
11. Kittle, "Folk Music," 195.
12. Aurora Lucero-White Lea, *Los Pastores* (Santa Fe: Santa Fe Press, Inc., 1940), Introduction.
13. Lea, *Los Pastores*, Introduction.
14. J. A. Carruth, compiler, *First Annual Directory of Las Vegas, New Mexico, for 1895–96* (Las Vegas, New Mexico: J. A. Carruth, 1895), 130.
15. Lucero-White, "*Coloquios*," vii-viii.

16. Early newspapers in Las Vegas include *La Voz del Pueblo* and *Revista Católica*.

Chapter 1

1. Howard Bryan, *Wildest of the Wild West* (Santa Fe, New Mexico: Clear Light Publishers, 1988), 100.
2. F. Stanley, *The Las Vegas (New Mexico) Story* (New Edition. Santa Fe: Sunstone Press, 2012.), 111. Also see LeGault, 6-8.
3. Dorothy Lea LeGault, "Footlights in the Foothills: A History of the Las Vegas, New Mexico, Opera Houses" (master's thesis, New Mexico Highlands University, 1971), 49.
4. *Daily Gazette* (Las Vegas), March 11, 1886. For a list of the various titles of the *Gazette,* see the bibliography section of Nicolás Kanellos and Helvetia Martell, *Hispanic Periodicals in the United States, Origins to 1960: A Brief History and Comprehensive Bibliography (Recovering the US Hispanic Literary Heritage).* Hereafter, this newspaper will be referred to as *Gazette.*
5. Perrigo, *Gateway,* 69.
6. LeGault, 10-11.
7. LeGault, 13-18.
8. LeGault, 25-29.
9. Harry L. Cutler, Insurance Agent, notes on reverse of "Big Fire at Las Vegas N. M. June 8, 1912", J. L. Tooker, photographer, 76.4.12, City of Las Vegas Museum and Rough Rider Collection, Las Vegas, New Mexico.
10. Marcus Gottschalk, "Lost Las Vegas Photo Exhibit," Citizens' Committee for Historic Preservation, www.lasvegasnmcchp.com/tours/lost/default.htm (accessed April 7, 2010).
11. *Daily Optic* (Las Vegas), December 27, 1879 quoted in Stanley, 115. Hereafter this newspaper will be referred to as *Optic.*
12. Perrigo, *Gateway,* 71-78.
13. Mark Lee Gardner, *To Hell on a Fast Horse, Billy the Kid, Pat Garrett, and the Epic Chase to Justice in the Old West* (New York: William Morrow, 2010), 7-12.
14. Bryan, 189.
15. *Gazette,* Mar 11, 1886.
16. *Optic* Sept 7, 1887.
17. Lynn I. Perrigo, "The Original Las Vegas, 1835–1935," [1975], MS 391, Southwest Collection, Carnegie Library, Las Vegas, New Mexico.
18. R. A. Kistler quoted in Perrigo, *Gateway,* 70.

19. Bryan, 124.
20. *Optic,* October 18, 1881.
21. *Optic*, December 10, 1879.
22. *Optic*, May 28, 1880.
23. Gardner, 120.
24. Perrigo, *Gateway* 24.
25. Milton W. Callon, *Las Vegas, New Mexico . . . The Town That Wouldn't Gamble* (Las Vegas: The Las Vegas Publishing Co. Inc., 1962), 48-49.
26. *Optic*, February 25, 1885.
27. Mark Bryan, "Magnificent Barbarism: The Rube and the Performance of the Rural on the American Vaudeville Stage, 1875–1925," abstract, Ohio State University ETDs, 2002, http://rave.ohiolink.edu/etdc/view?acc_num=osu1224269084 (accessed October 4, 2009).
28. Gerald Bordman, *American Theatre: A chronicle of Comedy and Drama, 1869–1914* (New York: Oxford UP, 1994), 123; 250.
29. *Optic,* Feb 24, 1885.
30. *Optic*, February 25, 1885.
31. *Optic*, February 27, 1885.
32. Gerald Bordman, *The Oxford Companion to American Theatre*, 3rd ed. (New York: Oxford UP, 2004), 153.
33. *Optic,* February 27, 1885.
34. *Optic*, March 3, 1885.
35. *Gazette,* March 5, 1886.
36. *Gazette,* March 5, 11, 13, 1886.
37. *Gazette,* March 28, 1886.
38. LeGault, 38.
39. American Libraries Text Archives, *Nevada, or, The lost mine: a drama in three acts,* www.archive.org/details/nevadaorlostmine00bakerich (accessed February 6, 2010).
40. *Optic,* July 3, 1893.
41. *Optic,* March 18, 1897.
42. Carruth, 137.
43. Jessie Couthoui Programme, April 30, 1890, City of Las Vegas Museum and Rough Rider Collection. 76.6.2.
44. *Optic*, July 6, 1894.
45. "Supplement to the Las Vegas Daily Optic. Building Edition," *Optic,* April 15, 1899, 20.
46. *Optic*, March 18, 1897.
47. *Optic*, advertisement, Jan 6, 1886; "The Union Spy" January 11, 1886.
48. *Optic,* January 11, 1886.
49. Robert M. Utley, *Fort Union National Monument* (Washington, DC: U. S. Government Printing Office, 1962), 27-31.
50. *Optic* January 11, 1886; Perrigo, "The Original," 389.

51. For discussion of minstrelsy, see Jon W. Finson, *The Voices That Are Gone: Themes in Nineteenth-Century American Popular Song* (New York: Oxford UP, 1997).

52. Allen L. Potts, Heritage Pursuit, 1998, *History of Hancock County Ohio,* Chapter 29, Village of Findlay (Chicago: Warner Beers & Co., 1886). http://heritagepursuit.com/Hancock/Hancockchapxxix.htm (accessed December 2, 2009).

53. Ethel McClure, "The Protestant Home A Pioneer Venture in Caring for the Aged," *Minnesota History Magazine*, 38, no. 2 (June 1962: 78, www.mnhs.org/market/mhspress/minnesotahistory/xml/v38i02.xml (accessed April 1, 2010).

54. *Optic*, January 11, 1886.

55. For dates of the play and author, see Open Library, *The Woven Web,* http://openlibrary.org/b/OL17807131M/woven_web (accessed December 21, 2009); for advertisement of performances in Las Vegas, New Mexico, see, *Optic,* July 3, 1894.

56. James Graham McNary, *This Is My Life* (Albuquerque: University of New Mexico Press, 1956), 21.

57. *Optic*, July 6, 1894.

58. Arellano, *Las Vegas Grandes*, 43-44; 22.

59. Anselmo Arellano, "The Rise of Mutual Aid Societies Among New Mexico's Spanish-Speaking During the Territorial Period" (Seminar Paper, New Mexico Highlands University, 1976), 23; Arellano, *Las Vegas Grandes*, 46-47; *La Voz del Pueblo*, November 14, 1891.

60. Arellano, *Las Vegas Grandes*, 23.

61. *La Voz del Pueblo*, February 6, 1892.

62. *La Voz del Pueblo*, March 5, 1892.

Chapter 2

1. Englekirk, 235; 254.

2. Lucero-White, vi-vii.

3. Englekirk, 235-36, 251; Lucero-White, vii.

4. Englekirk, 254.

5. John Donald Robb, "Folkpoets of Old Mexico," *New Mexico Magazine* (November–December 1966): 11.

6. United States Bureau of the Census, *Thirteenth Census of the United States: 1910* (Washington, DC: National Archives and Records Administration, 1910).

7. United States, Selective Service System, *World War I Selective Service System Draft Registration Cards, 1917–1918* (Washington, DC:

National Archives and Records Administration, M1509, 4,582 rolls).

8. Robb, 11.

9. For a complete list of plays in the Baca Troupe repertoire, see Englekirk, 235, n. 10.

10. Englekirk, 235, n. 10.

11. Englekirk, 235, n. 10.

12. Julián Josué Vigil, "King Arthur in New Mexico" (Las Vegas: Editorial Telaraña, 1981), 1.

13. A diligent search of daily editions of *Revista Católica* and *La Voz del Pueblo* of Las Vegas may reveal information on additional performances of the Baca Troupe.

14. Miguel Antonio Otero. *My Life on the Frontier 1882–1897.* (New Edition. Santa Fe: Sunstone Press), 2007, 32, 245.

15. Otero, 248.

16. Otero, 32.

17. Otero, 245, 248.

18. Otero, 32.

19. *Optic,* Hand's Music School advertisement, April 4, 1890.

20. "San Miguel National Bank is Second Oldest in City," *Las Vegas Daily Optic Boost and Build Edition* (Las Vegas: np, 1915), 23.

21. Otero, 248.

22. Perrigo, *Gateway,* 76, 70.

23. *Gazette,* February 24, 1886.

24. Otero, 248.

25. Perrigo, *Gateway,* 68.

26. *Merriam-Webster Online Dictionary,* www.merriam-webster.com/dictionary/opera bouffe (accessed March 20, 2010).

27. Bordman, *The Oxford Companion,* 182.

28. *Optic,* June 1, 1885.

29. advertisement *Optic,* March 5, 1898.

30. Perrigo, "The Original," 388.

31. *Optic,* June 3, 1885.

32. "Chilpéric (operetta)," http://en.wikipedia.org/wiki/Chilp%C3%A9ric_(operetta). (accessed November 28, 2009).

33. "A Brilliant Success," *Optic,* Mar 7, 1886.

34. *Gazette,* Mar 7, 1886.

35. "The Opera," *Gazette,* March 3, 1886.

36. *Gazette,* March 7, 1886.

37. *Gazette,* February 28, 1886.

38. "The Opera," *Gazette,* Mar 9, 1886.

39. LeGault, 23-24.

40. *Gazette,* March 9, 1886.

41. Allardyce Nicoll, *A History of English Drama 1660–1900, Vol. V*

Late Nineteenth Century Drama 1850–1900 (Cambridge: University Printing House, 1967), 580.

42. "Amusements," *Optic*, January 19, 1887.
43. *Optic*, January 19, 1887.
44. *Optic,* January 19, 1887.
45. Otero, 42.
46. *Optic,* January 19, 1886.
47. Otero, 41.
48. The Las Vegas Opera Troupe, *Billee Taylor* Souvenir Program, January 21, 1887 (Archives of the City of Las Vegas Museum and Rough Rider Memorial Collection, 76.6.1).
49. "Criticisms of Billee Taylor," *Optic,* January 22, 1887.
50. *Optic,* January 22, 1887.
51. Bordman, *The Oxford Companion,* 394.
52. *Optic,* April 8, 1890.
53. *Optic,* April 9, 1890.
54. *Optic,* April 9, 1890.
55. Oscar G. Brockett, *History of the Theatre* (Boston: Allyn and Bacon, Inc., 1982), 501.
56. "The Mikado," *Optic,* November 13, 1890.
57. *Optic,* June 11, 1892.
58. *Optic,* June 11, 1892.
59. *Optic,* June 8 and 9, 1892.
60. *Optic,* June 9, 1892; Carruth, 116.
61. *Optic,* June 9, 1892.
62. *Optic,* June 10 and June 11, 1892.
63. Advertisement, *Optic,* August 4, 1887.
64. "Hook and Ladder Benefit" Advertisement, *Optic,* April 12, 1890 and April 14, 1890.
65. "Seventh Recital Given by the Pupils of Hand's Music School Assisted by the Las Vegas Opera Company." Program, June 18, 1890, Courtesy City of Las Vegas Museum and Rough Rider Memorial Collection.
66. *Optic,* February 17, 1894.
67. Brockett, 500.
68. LeGault, 68.
69. *Optic,* April 7, 1894.
70. Brockett, 499-500.
71. "A Pointed Appeal," *Optic,* November 8, 1895.
72. "A Pointed Appeal," *Optic,* November 8, 1890.
73. *The Las Vegas Daily Optic.* Building Edition (East Las Vegas, New Mexico: April, 1899), 6.
74. Ibid., 16.
75. *Optic,* November 8, 1895.

76. "A Great Success," *Optic,* November 12, 1895.
77. "Little Lord Fauntleroy," *The New York Times,* October 21, 1898. www.nytimes.com/ref/membercenter/nytarchive.html (accessed March 6, 2010).
78. "A Great Success," *Optic,* November 12, 1895.
79. U.S. Bureau of the Census, *Twelfth Census of the United States, 1900.*

Chapter 3

1. Robert M. Utley, *Fort Union National Monument* (Washington, DC: United States Government Printing Office, 1962), 9-10.
2. Utley, 18.
3. Utley, 52.
4. Utley, 10-11.
5. Dale F. Giese, "Social Life at Fort Union, New Mexico in the 1880s" (master's thesis, New Mexico Highlands University, 1964), 53-57.
6. quoted in F. Stanley, *Fort Union (New Mexico)* (Denver: World Press, 1953), 206-207.
7. *Gazette,* March 13th, 1883.
8. *Optic,* October 9, 1883.
9. *Optic,* Oct 9, 1883.
10. In spite of several searches with Fort Union National Monument staff as recently as late 2009 and extensive research of both primary and secondary sources, the location of a building designated as an opera house has not been found. See also discussion in Dale Frederick Giese, "Social Life at Fort Union, New Mexico in the 1880s," 57 and 79.
11. "The Coming Comedy Company," *Optic,* October 16, 1883.
12. Finson, 224-5, 193.
13. *Optic,* October 16, 1883.
14. *Optic,* October 17, 1883.
15. *Optic* October 18, 1883.
16. Stanley, *Fort Union,* 208-09.
17. *Optic,* October 18, 1883.
18. Stanley, *Fort Union,* 208.
19. Giese, 31.
20. *Optic,* October 19, 1883.
21. Stanley, *Fort Union (New Mexico),* 209.
22. *Optic,* October 18, 1883.
23. *Optic,* October 19, 1883.
24. "Our Fort Union Letter," *Optic,* October 22, 1883.
25. *Optic,* October 16, 1883.

26. Perrigo, *Gateway,* 70.

27. "Our Fort Union Letter," *Optic,* January 15, 1884.

28. quoted in Stanley, *Fort Union (New Mexico)*, 213.

29. quoted in Stanley, *Fort Union (New Mexico)*, 213.

30. *Optic,* January 15, 1884.

31. "Fritz Emmet Sobering Up," *New York Times,* April 21, 1890, http:// query.nytimes.com/gst/abstract.html?res=940DE4D6153BE533A25752 C2A9629C94619ED7CF (accessed May 25, 2009).

32. Stanley, *Fort Union (New Mexico)*, 213.

33. Hal Erickson, Review Summary, Maude Muller (1909), *New York Times,* http://movies.nytimes.com/movie/241884/Maude-Muller/overview (accessed May 25, 2009).

34. Stanley, *Fort Union (New Mexico),* 214.

35. *Optic,* January 15, 1884.

36. Mark Blagrave, "Temperance and the Theatre in the Nineteenth Century Maritimes," *Theatre Research in Canada* vol. 17 no. 1 (Spring 1986): 23-32.

37. *Optic,* January 15, 1884; Giese, 33.

38. *Optic,* January 15, 1884.

39. *Optic,* February 16, 1884.

40. *Optic,* March 27, 1884.

41. *Optic,* April 17, 1884.

42. *Optic,* April 17, 1884.

43. *Optic,* April 29, 1884.

44. *Optic,* April 29, 1884.

45. *Optic,* April 29, 1884; this quotation and the previous three paragraphs of information are found in Gus's letter of April 29, 1884, in the *Optic.*

46. "Military Change," *Optic,* May 8, 1884.

47. *Optic,* April 29, 1884.

48. Stanley, 205.

49. Giese, 114, 35.

50. Finson, 224-225; for an image of Harrigan and Hart as "The Mulligan Guard," see Finson, illustration 8.3.

51. Giese, 35-36.

52. *Optic,* July 2, 1885.

53. Finson, 182; for the lyrics to "Ben Bolt," see www.contemplator.com/ America/bbolt.html (retrieved January 29, 2010).

54. *Optic,* October 30, 1885.

55. *Optic,* October 30, 1885.

56. *Gazette,* February 17,1886; as noted in Chapter 2, the author of "Our Boys" was H. J. Byron.

57. Giese, 38.

Epilogue

1. LeGault, 25-26.
2. Las Vegas Oratorio Society. Program from Music Festival: "The Creation" (Las Vegas: Las Vegas Publishing Company, 1899). City of Las Vegas Museum and Rough Rider Collection, 2006.24.6.
3. "The Musical Festival," *Optic,* June 24, 1899.
4. "The Musical Festival," *Optic,* June 24, 1899.
5. James Graham McNary, *This Is My Life* (Albuquerque: University of New Mexico Press, 1956), 16.
6. "The Musical Festival," *Optic,* June 24, 1899.
7. Supplement to the *Las Vegas Daily Optic.* Building Edition (East Las Vegas: Las Vegas Publishing Company, 1899), 3.
8. Frank White Johnson, Eugene C. Barker, Ernest William Winkler, *A History of Texas and Texans Volume 4* (Chicago: The American Historical Society, 1914), 1604-05.
9. McNary, 41-47.
10. *Optic,* June 24, 1899.
11. The Hand Concert Co. program, City of Las Vegas Museum and Rough Rider Memorial Collection.
12. George H. Wilson and Calvin B. Cody, eds., *Musical Yearbook of the United States,* Volume 8-10 (Chicago: Clayton F. Summy, 1893), 79.
13. L. Von Meyerhoff to Harriet Knickerbocker, January 23, 1888, City of Las Vegas Museum and Rough Rider Memorial Collection, 76.6.2.
14. *Optic,* June 24, 1899.
15. Official Program, First Annual Reunion Roosevelt's Rough Riders, Jun 24–26, 1899, Las Vegas, New Mexico. Rough Riders' Reunion Collection, City of Las Vegas Museum and Rough Rider Memorial Collection, 102.01.03.
16. McNary, 23.
17. "Revised Program of the Festivities," *La Voz del Pueblo*, Sat June 24, 1899, trans. Benito G. Duran (unpublished paper, New Mexico Highlands University), Rough Riders' Memorial Collection, City of Las Vegas Museum and Rough Rider Memorial Collection, 102.01.07.
18. "Minstrels Tonight," *Optic,* November 6, 1899; LeGault, 72.
19. Perrigo, "The Original," 391.
20. Otero quoted in Howard Bryan, Illustration Miguel A. Otero, *Wildest of the Wild West* (Santa Fe: Clear Light Publishers, 1988).

Resources

Archival Material

City of Las Vegas Museum and Rough Rider Memorial Collection, Las Vegas, New Mexico.
Fort Union National Monument, New Mexico.

Books, Articles, and Letters

American Libraries Text Archives. *Nevada, or, The lost mine: a drama in three acts.* www.archive.org/details/nevadaorlostmine00bakerich (accessed February 6, 2010).

Arellano, Anselmo. "The Rise of Mutual Aid Societies Among New Mexico's Spanish-Speaking During the Territorial Period." Seminar Paper, New Mexico Highlands University,1976.

Arellano, Anselmo and Julián Josué Vigil. *Las Vegas Grandes on the Gallinas 1835–1985.* Las Vegas, New Mexico: Editorial Teleraña, 1985.

Blagrave, Mark. "Temperance and the Theatre in the Nineteenth Century Maritimes." *Theatre Research in Canada.* vol. 7 no 1 (Spring 1986). 23-32.

Bordman, Gerald. *American Theatre: A Chronicle of Comedy and Drama, 1869–1914.* New York: Oxford University Press, 1994.

Bordman, Gerald Martin. *The Oxford Companion to American Theatre.* New York: Oxford University Press, 2004. 3rd Edition.

Brockett, Oscar G. *History of the Theatre.* 4th Edition. Boston: Allyn and Bacon, Inc., 1982.

Bryan, Howard. *Wildest of the Wild West.* Santa Fe: Clear Light Publishers, 1988.

Bryan, Mark Evans. "Magnificent Barbarism: The Rube and the Performance of the Rural on the American Vaudeville Stage, 1875–1925." Abstract. Ohio State University ETDs, 2002. rave.ohiolink.edu/etdc/view?acc_num=osu1224269084 (accessed October 4, 2009).

Callon, Milton W. *Las Vegas, New Mexico . . . The Town That Wouldn't Gamble.* Las Vegas: The Las Vegas Publishing Co. Inc.; *Las Vegas Daily Optic,* 1962.

Carruth, J. A. *First Annual Directory of Las Vegas, New Mexico, for 1895–96.* Las Vegas, New Mexico: J. A. Carruth, Printer and Binder, 1895.

"Chilpéric (operetta)." http://en.wikipedia.org/wiki/Chilp%C3%A9ric_(operetta) (accessed November 28, 2009).

Englekirk, John E. "The Source and Dating of New Mexico Spanish Folk Plays." *Western Folklore.* Oct 1957. 232-255.

Finson, Jon W. *The Voices That Are Gone: Themes in Nineteenth-Century American Popular Song.* USA: Oxford UP, 1997.

Gardner, Mark. *To Hell on a Fast Horse, Billy the Kid, Pat Garrett, and the Epic Chase to Justice in the Old West.* New York: William Morrow, An Imprint of Harper Collins Publishers, 2010.

Giese, Dale F. "Social Life at Fort Union, New Mexico in the 1880s." Master's Thesis, New Mexico Highlands University, 1964.

Gottschalk, Marcus. "Lost Las Vegas Photo Exhibit." Citizens' Committee for Historic Preservation. www.lasvegasnmcchp.com/tours/lost/default.htm (accessed April 7, 2010).

Gregg, Andrew K. *New Mexico in the Nineteenth Century A Pictorial History*. Albuquerque: University of New Mexico Press, 1968.

Johnson, Frank White, Eugene C. Barker, and Ernest William Winkler. *A History of Texas and Texans*, Volume 4. Chicago: The American Historical Society, 1914.

Kanellos, Nicolás and Helvetia Martell. *Hispanic Periodicals in the United States, Origins to 1960: A Brief History and Comprehensive Bibliography (Recovering the US Hispanic Literary Heritage)*. Houston: Arte Publico Press, 2000.

Kittle, J. L. "Folk Music of the Upper Rio Grande." *Southwest Review* 30 (1945): 192-95.

Lea, Aurora Lucero-White. *Literary Folklore of the Hispanic Southwest*. San Antonio: The Naylor Company, 1953.

_____. *Coloquios de Los Pastores*. Santa Fe: Santa Fe Press, Inc. 1940.

LeGault, Dorothy Lea. "Footlights in the Foothills: A History of the Las Vegas, New Mexico, Opera Houses." Master's Thesis, New Mexico Highlands University, 1971.

"Little Lord Fauntleroy." *The New York Times* October 21, 1898. www.nytimes.com/ref/membercenter/nytarchive.html (accessed March 6, 2010).

Lucero-White, Aurora. "*Coloquios de los pastores de Las Vegas*." Master's Thesis, New Mexico Normal University, 1932.

McClure, Ethel. "The Protestant Home of St. Paul A Pioneer Venture in Caring for the Aged." *Minnesota History Magazine* 38, 2 (June 1962): 74-85. www.mnhs.org/market/mhspress/minnesotahistory/xml/v38i02.xml (accessed April 1, 2010).

McNary, James Graham. *This Is My Life*. Albuquerque: University of New Mexico Press, 1956.

Nicoll, Allardyce. *A History of English Drama 1660–1900. vol. V Late Nineteenth Century Drama 1850–1900*. Cambridge: University Printing House, 1967.

Open Library. *The Woven Web.* http://openlibrary.org/b/OL17807131M/ woven_web (accessed April 1, 2010).

opera bouffe. (2010). In Merriam-Webster Online Dictionary. www. Merriam-webster.com/dictionary/opera bouffe (accessed March 20, 2010).

Otero, Miguel Antonio. *My Life on the Frontier 1882–1897.* New Edition. Santa Fe: Sunstone Press, 2007.

Perrigo, Lynn. *Gateway to Glorieta, A History of Las Vegas, New Mexico.* New Edition. Santa Fe: Sunstone Press, 2010.

_____. "The Original Las Vegas, 1835–1935." Las Vegas, 1975. Unpublished Ms., Carnegie Library, Southwest Collection.

Potts, Allen L. Heritage Pursuit, 1998. "Village of Findlay." History of Hancock County Ohio. Chicago: Warner Beers & Co., 1886. http:// heritagepursuit.com/Hancock/Hancockchapxxix.htm (accessed December 2, 2009).

Robb, John Donald. "Folkpoets of Old Mexico." *New Mexico Magazine.* (November–December 1966): 10-12.

Stanley, F. *Fort Union (New Mexico).* New Edition. Santa Fe: Sunstone Press, 2012.

_____. *The Las Vegas, (New Mexico), Story.* New Edition. Santa Fe: Sunstone Press, 2010.

United States Bureau of the Census. *Thirteenth Census of the United States: 1910* (Washington, D C: National Archives and Records Administration, 1910).

United States, Selective Service System, World War I Selective Service System Draft Registration Cards, 1917–1918 (Washington, DC: National Archives and Records Administration, M1509, 4,582 rolls).

Utley, Robert M. *Fort Union National Monument.* Washington, DC: United States Government Printing Office, 1962.

Vigil, Julián Josué. *King Arthur in New Mexico.* Las Vegas: Editorial Teleraña, 1981.

Wilson, George H. and Calvin B. Cady, eds. *Musical Yearbook of the United States*, Volume 8-10. Chicago: Clayton F. Summy, 1893.

Newspapers

Daily Gazette, Las Vegas, New Mexico
La Voz del Pueblo, Las Vegas, New Mexico
Las Vegas Daily Optic, New Mexico
New York Times Online Archive
Revista Católica, Las Vegas, New Mexico

Index

Plays, Players, Playwrights, and Venues

Page numbers in italic text indicate illustrations.

www.ingramcontent.com/pod-product-compliance
Lightning Source LLC
Chambersburg PA
CBHW031145090426
42738CB00008B/1226